Easy
Slow Cooker
COOKBOOK

Barbara C. Jones

Published by Cookbook Resources, LLC

Easy Slow Cooker Cookbook
Simple Ingredients and Easy Preparation for Hassle-Free Cooking

1st Printing - April 2004
2nd Printing - November 2004
3rd Printing - July 2005
4th Printing - September 2005
5th Printing - November 2005
6th Printing - January 2006
7th Printing - June 2006
8th Printing - April 2007
9th Printing - November 2007
10th Printing - March 2009
11th Printing - August 2009
12th Printing - April 2010

International Standard Book Number: 978-1-931294-45-4

Library of Congress Control Number: 2003105100

Library of Congress Catalog Data:

Jones, Barbara C.
  Easy slow cooker cookbook / Barbara C. Jones. Portion of Title: Slow cooker cookbook
  286 p. : ill. ; 24 cm.
  ISBN: 1931294445
  Includes index.
  Subjects: Electric cookery, Slow.
  TX827 .J65 2003
  641.5/884 22
  pcc

Illustrations by Nancy Murphy Griffith
Edited, Designed, Published and Manufactured in the
United States of America by
Cookbook Resources, LLC
541 Doubletree Drive
Highland Village, Texas 75077

Toll free 866-229-2665

www.cookbookresources.com

Bringing Family and Friends to the Table

This cookbook is dedicated with gratitude and respect to all cooks who bring families to the table for homecooked meals.

Table of

Contents

INTRODUCTION

Born of necessity, these convenient slow cookers make life easier for anyone who uses them. Put your food inside, cover the pot, turn the switch to "on" and come home after hours of errands, soccer games, meetings, work or play and dinner is ready! Meals are simple, convenient and much better than any fast-food, drive-through-window meal.

Easy Slow Cooker Cookbook provides recipes for beef, chicken, seafood, vegetables, soups and casseroles that are great as 1-DISH MEALS or accompaniments with a main dish.

These recipes are family tested and used everyday by moms, dads, seniors, teens and college students. They are packed with nutritious ingredients, economical, wholesome and practical.

The recipes are easy, simple and everyday cooking that everybody loves. They are ones families grow up on and ones we remember long after adulthood. They are recipes that give you a warm and fuzzy feeling and let you know someone cares about you.

These recipes should never be taken for granted, passed by because they are too simple or too "normal". They are the recipes that strengthen our families and bring us the happiness and satisfaction of being together for a homecooked meal.

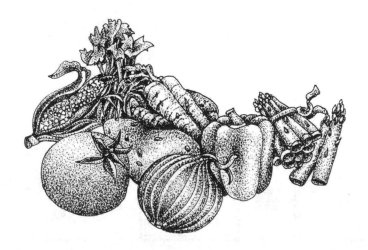

APPETIZERS

Unbelievable Crab Dip

1 (6 ounce) can white crabmeat, drained, flaked	2 (168 g)
1 (8 ounce) package cream cheese, softened	227 g
½ cup (1 stick) butter, sliced	120 ml
2 tablespoons white cooking wine	30 ml

- Combine crabmeat, cream cheese, butter and wine in sprayed, small slow cooker.

- Cover and cook on LOW for 1 hour and gently stir to combine all ingredients. Serve from cooker with chips or crackers. Serves 4 to 6.

Crab Dip

1 (8 ounce) and 1 (3 ounce) packages cream cheese, softened	227 g/84 g
⅔ cup mayonnaise	160 ml
1 tablespoon white wine Worcestershire sauce	15 ml
1 tablespoon sherry or cooking sherry	15 ml
3 fresh green onions with tops, chopped	
2 (6 ounce) cans crabmeat, drained, flaked	2 (168 g)

- Spray, small slow cooker. In bowl, combine cream cheese, mayonnaise, 1 teaspoon (5 ml) salt and Worcestershire and mix well with fork.

- Stir in sherry, onions and crabmeat and spoon into slow cooker.

- Cover, cook on LOW for 1 hour 30 minutes to 2 hours and stir once. Serves 6 to 8.

Broccoli Dip

¾ cup (1½ sticks) butter	180 ml
2 cups thinly sliced celery	480 ml
1 onion, finely chopped	
3 tablespoons flour	45 ml
1 (10 ounce) can cream of chicken soup	280 g
1 (10 ounce) box chopped broccoli, thawed	280 g
1 (5 ounce) garlic cheese roll, cut in chunks	143 g

- In skillet, melt butter and saute celery and onion, but do not brown; stir in flour.

- Spoon into small slow cooker, stir in remaining ingredients and mix well.

- Cover and cook on LOW for 2 to 3 hours and stir several times.

- Serve with wheat crackers or corn chips. Serves 6 to 8.

Cheesy Bacon Dip

2 (8 ounce) packages cream cheese, softened	2 (227 g)
1 (8 ounce) package shredded colby Jack cheese	227 g
2 tablespoons mustard	30 ml
2 teaspoons white Worcestershire sauce	30 ml
4 fresh green onions with tops, sliced	
1 pound bacon, cooked, crumbled	.5 kg

- Cut cream cheese into cubes and place in 4 or 5-quart slow cooker.

- Add colby Jack cheese, mustard, white Worcestershire, green onions and ¼ teaspoon (1 ml) salt.

- Cover, cook on LOW for 1 hour and stir to melt cheese.

- Stir in crumbled bacon. Serve with small-size rye bread or toasted pumpernickel bread. Serves 6 to 8.

Hamburger Dip
Men love this meaty, spicy dip.

2 pounds lean ground beef	1 kg
2 tablespoons dried minced onion	30 ml
1½ teaspoons dried oregano leaves	7 ml
1 tablespoon chili powder	15 ml
2 teaspoons sugar	10 ml
1 (10 ounce) can tomatoes and green chilies	280 g
½ cup chili sauce	120 ml
2 (16 ounce) packages cubed Mexican Velveeta® cheese	2 (.5 kg)

- In large skillet, brown ground beef, drain and transfer to sprayed 4 to 5-quart (4 L) slow cooker.

- Add remaining ingredients plus ½ to 1 cup (240 ml) water and stir well.

- Cover, cook on LOW for 1 hour 30 minutes to 2 hours. Stir once or twice during cooking time. Add a little salt, if desired. Serve hot with chips or spread on crackers. Serves 8 to 10.

Hot Broccoli Dip

1 (16 ounce) box Mexican Velveeta® cheese, cubed	.5 kg
1 (10 ounce) can golden mushroom soup	280 g
¼ cup milk	60 ml
1 (10 ounce) box frozen chopped broccoli, thawed	280 g

- In sprayed slow cooker, combine cheese, soup and milk, stir well and fold in broccoli.

- Cover and cook on LOW for 1 to 2 hours. Stir before serving. Serves 8 to 10.

Chicken-Enchilada Dip

2 pounds boneless, skinless chicken thighs, cubed	1 kg
1 (10 ounce) can enchilada sauce	280 g
1 (7 ounce) can chopped green chilies, drained	196 g
1 small onion, finely chopped	
1 large sweet red bell pepper, finely chopped	
2 (8 ounce) packages cream cheese, cubed	2 (227 g)
1 (16 ounce) package shredded American cheese	.5 kg

- In sprayed 4 to 5-quart (5 L) slow cooker, place chicken thighs, enchilada sauce, green chilies, onion and bell pepper.

- Cover and cook on LOW for 4 to 6 hours. Stir in cream cheese and American cheese and cook additional 30 minutes. Stir several times during cooking. Serve with tortilla chips. Serves 8 to 10.

Indian-Corn Dip

1 pound lean ground beef	.5 kg
1 onion, finely chopped	
1 (15 ounce) can whole kernel corn, drained	425 g
1 (16 ounce) jar salsa	425 g
1 (1 pound) package cubed Velveeta® cheese	.5 kg

- In skillet, brown and cook grounded beef on low heat for about 10 minutes and drain.

- Transfer to slow cooker and add onion, corn, salsa and cheese. Cover and cook on LOW for 1 hour, remove lid and stir. Serve with tortilla chips. Serves 6 to 8.

Pepperoni Dip

1 (6 ounce) package pepperoni	168 g
1 bunch fresh green onions, thinly sliced	
½ sweet red bell pepper, finely chopped	
1 medium tomato, finely chopped	
1 (14 ounce) jar pizza sauce	396 g
1½ cups shredded mozzarella cheese	360 ml
1 (8 ounce) package cream cheese, cubed	227 g

- Chop pepperoni into small pieces and place in small slow cooker. Add onion, bell pepper, tomato and pizza sauce and stir well.

- Cover and cook on LOW for 2 hours 30 minutes to 3 hours 30 minutes. Stir in mozzarella and cream cheese and stir until they melt.

- Serve with wheat crackers or tortilla chips. Serves 4 to 6.

Sausage-Hamburger Dip

1 pound bulk pork sausage	.5 kg
1 pound lean ground beef	.5 kg
1 cup hot salsa	240 ml
1 (10 ounce) can cream of mushroom soup	280 g
1 (10 ounce) can tomatoes and green chilies	280 g
1 teaspoon garlic powder	5 ml
¾ teaspoon ground oregano	4 ml
2 (16 ounce) packages cubed Velveeta® cheese	2 (.5 kg)

- In large skillet, brown, cook sausage and ground beef for 15 minutes and drain.

- Place in sprayed 4 to 5-quart (4 L) slow cooker.

- Add salsa, mushroom soup, tomatoes, green chilies, garlic powder and oregano and stir well. Fold in cheese.

- Cover and cook on LOW for 1 hour or until cheese melts. Stir once during cooking time.

- Serve from cooker. Serves 8 to 10.

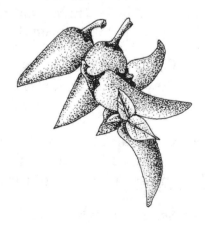

Whiz Bang Dip

1 pound lean ground beef	.5 kg
1 small onion, very finely chopped	
2 (16 ounce) package cubed Velveeta® cheese	2 (.5 kg)
2 (10 ounce) cans chopped tomatoes	
and green chilies	2 (280 g)
1 teaspoon minced garlic	5 ml

- In skillet, cook beef on low heat for 10 minutes and break up large meat chunks. Transfer to 4-quart (4 L) slow cooker and add onion, cheese, tomatoes and green chilies and garlic.

- Stir well, cover and cook on LOW for 1 hour. Serve with tortilla chips. Serves 6 to 8.

The Big Dipper

2 (15 ounce) cans chili	2 (425 g)
1 (10 ounce) can tomatoes and green chilies	280 g
1 (16 ounce) package cubed Velveeta® cheese	.5 kg
1 bunch fresh green onions, chopped	

- Place all ingredients in slow cooker and cook on LOW for 1 hour to 1 hour 30 minutes.

- Serve right from slow cooker. Stir before serving. Serves 6 to 8.

Firecrackers and Bacon

1 (16 ounce) package cubed Mexican Velveeta® cheese	.5 kg
1 (10 ounce) can tomatoes and green chilies	280 g
1 tablespoon dry minced onion	15 ml
2 teaspoons Worcestershire sauce	10 ml
½ teaspoon dried mustard	2 ml
½ cup whipping cream or half-and-half cream	120 ml
16 slices bacon, cooked, crumbled, divided	

- Lightly spray, small slow cooker and add cubed cheese, tomatoes and green chilies, onion, Worcestershire, mustard and cream.

- Turn heat to LOW, cover and cook about 1 hour, stirring several times to make sure cheese melts.

- While cheese is melting, place bacon in skillet, fry, drain and crumble.

- Fold three-fourths of bacon into cheese mixture. When ready to "dip", sprinkle remaining bacon on top and serve from slow cooker. Serves 4 to 6.

Great Balls of Fire

1 pound hot sausage	**.5 kg**
1 (10 ounce) can chopped tomatoes	
and green chilies	**280 g**
1 (2 pound) box Velveeta° cheese	**1 kg**

- In skillet, brown and cook sausage, drain and place in small, sprayed slow cooker.

- Stir in chopped tomatoes and green chilies and mix well.

- Cut cheese into chunks and add to sausage-tomato mixture.

- Cover and cook on LOW for 1 hour or until cheese melts.

- Stir when ready to serve and serve hot in slow cooker. Serves 4 to 6.

TIP: This works best with large tortilla chips.

Hot Reuben Spread

1 (8 ounce) package shredded Swiss cheese	227 g
¾ cup drained sauerkraut, rinsed, drained	180 ml
1 (8 ounce) package cream cheese, softened, cubed	227 g
2 (2.5 ounce) packages sliced corned beef, chopped	2 (70 g)

- Spray, small slow cooker.

- In bowl, combine Swiss cheese, sauerkraut, cream cheese and corned beef and spoon into slow cooker.

- Cover and cook on LOW for 1 hour.

- Serve on slices of 3-inch (8 cm) rye bread. Serves 4 to 6.

Crab-Artichoke Spread

1 (6 ounce) can crabmeat, flaked	168 g
½ cup grated parmesan cheese	120 ml
1 bunch fresh green onions, sliced	
1½ tablespoons lemon juice	22 ml
1 (15 ounce) can artichoke hearts, drained, finely chopped	425 g
1 (8 ounce) package cream cheese, cubed	227 g

- Spray, small slow cooker, combine all ingredients and stir well.

- Cover and cook on LOW for 1 hour to 1 hour 30 minutes. Stir until cream cheese mixes well. Serve on toasted bagel chips. Serves 4 to 6.

Sausage-Pineapple Bits

The "sweet and hot" makes a delicious combo.

1 (1 pound) link cooked Polish sausage, skinned	.5 kg
1 (1 pound) hot bulk sausage	.5 kg
1 (8 ounce) can crushed pineapple with juice	227 g
1 cup apricot preserves	240 ml
1 tablespoon white wine Worcestershire sauce	15 ml
1½ cups packed brown sugar	360 ml

- Slice link sausage into ½-inch (1.2 cm) pieces. Shape bulk sausage into 1-inch (2.5 cm) balls and brown in skillet.

- In slow cooker, place sausage pieces, sausage balls, pineapple, apricot preserves, Worcestershire sauce and brown sugar. Stir gently so meatballs do not break up.

- Cover and cook on LOW for 1 hour 30 minutes to 2 hours. Serves 8 to 10.

Party Smokies

1 cup ketchup	240 ml
1 cup plum jelly	240 ml
1 tablespoon lemon juice	15 ml
2 (5 ounce) packages tiny smoked sausages	2 (143 g)

- Combine all ingredients in small, sprayed slow cooker. Cover and cook on LOW for 1 hour.

- Stir before serving. Serve right from cooker. Serves 4 to 6.

Teriyaki Wingettes

2½ pounds chicken wingettes	**1.2 kg**
1 onion, chopped	
1 cup soy sauce	**240 ml**
1 cup packed brown sugar	**240 ml**
1 teaspoon minced garlic	**5 ml**
1½ teaspoons ground ginger	**7 ml**

- Rinse chicken and pat dry. Place chicken wingettes on broiler pan and broil about 10 minutes on both sides.

- Transfer wingettes to large slow cooker.

- Combine onion, soy sauce, brown sugar, garlic and ginger. Spoon sauce over wingettes.

- Cook on HIGH for 2 hours. Stir wingettes once during cooking to coat chicken evenly with sauce. Serves 8 to 10.

Wingettes in Honey Sauce

1 (2 pound) package chicken wingettes	1 kg
2 cups honey	480 ml
¾ cup soy sauce	180 ml
¾ cup chili sauce	180 ml
¼ cup oil	60 ml
1 teaspoon minced garlic	5 ml
Dried parsley flakes, optional	

- Rinse chicken, pat dry and sprinkle with a little salt and pepper.

- Place wingettes in broiler pan and broil for 20 minutes (10 minutes on each side) or until light brown.

- Transfer to sprayed slow cooker.

- In bowl, combine honey, soy sauce, chili sauce, oil and garlic and spoon over wingettes.

- Cover and cook on LOW for 4 to 5 hours or on HIGH for 2 hours to 2 hours 30 minutes. Garnish with dried parsley flakes, if desired. Serves 8 to 10.

Spicy Franks

1 cup packed brown sugar	240 ml
1 cup chili sauce	240 ml
1 tablespoon red wine vinegar	15 ml
2 teaspoons soy sauce	10 ml
2 teaspoons dijon-style mustard	10 ml
2 (12 ounce) packages frankfurters	2 (340 g)

- Spray small slow cooker, combine brown sugar, chili sauce, vinegar, soy sauce and mustard and mix well. Cut frankfurters diagonally in 1-inch (2.5 cm) pieces. Stir in frankfurters.

- Cover and cook on LOW for 1 to 2 hours.

- Serve from cooker using cocktail picks. Serves 4.

Bubbly Franks

1 (1 pound) package wieners	.5 kg
½ cup chili sauce	120 ml
⅔ cup packed brown sugar	160 ml
½ cup bourbon	120 ml

- Cut wieners diagonally into bite-size pieces. Combine chili sauce, sugar and bourbon in small slow cooker.

- Stir in wieners and cook on LOW for 1 to 2 hours.

- Serve in chafing dish. Serves 6 to 8.

SOUPS, STEWS, CHOWDERS & JAMBALAYA

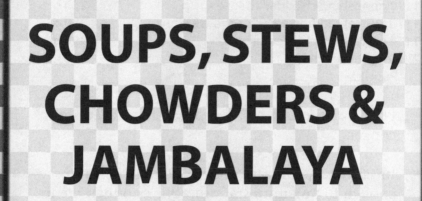

Potato Soup Plus!

5 medium potatoes, peeled, cubed	
2 cups cooked, cubed ham	480 ml
1 cup fresh broccoli florets, cut very, very fine	240 ml
1 (10 ounce) can cheddar cheese soup	280 g
1 (10 ounce) can fiesta nacho cheese soup	280 g
1 (14 ounce) can chicken broth	396 g
2½ soup cans milk	600 ml
Paprika	

- Place potatoes, ham and broccoli in sprayed slow cooker.

- In saucepan, combine soups and milk. Heat just enough to mix until smooth. Stir into ingredients already in slow cooker.

- Cover and cook on LOW for 7 to 9 hours.

- When serving, sprinkle a little paprika over each serving. Serves 6 to 8.

Mexican-Meatball Soup

3 (14 ounce) cans beef broth	3 (396 g)
1 (16 ounce) jar hot salsa	.5 kg
1 (16 ounce) package frozen whole kernel corn, thawed	.5 kg
1 (16 ounce) package frozen meatballs, thawed	.5 kg
1 teaspoon minced garlic	5 ml

- Combine all ingredients in slow cooker and stir well.

- Cover and cook on LOW for 5 to 7 hours. Serves 6 to 8.

Tasty Chicken and Rice Soup

1 pound boneless, skinless chicken breasts	.5 kg
½ cup brown rice	120 ml
1 (10 ounce) can cream of chicken soup	280 g
1 (10 ounce) can cream of celery soup	280 g
1 (14 ounce) can chicken broth with roasted garlic	396 g
1 (16 ounce) package frozen sliced carrots, thawed	.5 kg
1 cup half-and-half cream	240 ml

- Cut chicken into 1-inch pieces. Place pieces in sprayed 4 or 5-quart (4 L) slow cooker.

- In bowl, combine and mix rice, both soups, chicken broth and carrots and pour over chicken.

- Cover and cook on LOW 7 to 8 hours.

- Turn heat to HIGH, add half-and-half cream and cook additional 15 to 20 minutes. Serves 6 to 8.

Taco Soup

1½ pounds lean ground beef	.7 kg
1 (1 ounce) packet taco seasoning	28 g
2 (15 ounce) cans Mexican stewed tomatoes	2 (425 g)
2 (15 ounce) cans chili beans with liquid	2 (4205g)
1 (15 ounce) can whole kernel corn, drained	425 g
Crushed tortilla chips	
Shredded cheddar cheese	

- In skillet, brown ground beef until it is no longer pink. Place in 5 to 6-quart (5 L) slow cooker.

- Add taco seasoning, tomatoes, chili beans and 1 cup (240 ml) water and mix well.

- Cover and cook on LOW for 4 hours or on HIGH for 1 to 2 hours.

- Serve over crushed tortilla chips and sprinkle some shredded cheddar cheese over top of each serving. Serves 6 to 8.

Taco Soup Olé

2 pounds lean ground beef	**1 kg**
2 (15 ounce) cans ranch-style beans with liquid	**2 (425 g)**
1 (15 ounce) can whole kernel corn, drained	**425 g**
2 (15 ounce) cans stewed tomatoes	**2 (425 g)**
1 (10 ounce) can tomatoes and green chilies	**280 g**
1 (1 ounce) packet ranch dressing mix	**28 g**
1 (1 ounce) packet taco seasoning	**28 g**

- In large skillet, brown ground beef, drain and transfer to slow cooker.

- Add remaining ingredients and stir well.

- Cover and cook on LOW for 8 to 10 hours. Serves 6 to 8.

TIP: When serving, sprinkle shredded cheddar cheese over each serving.

Taco-Chili Soup

2 pounds very lean stew meat	1 kg
2 (15 ounce) cans Mexican stewed tomatoes	2 (425 g)
1 (1 ounce) packet taco seasoning mix	28 g
2 (15 ounce) cans pinto beans with liquid	2 (425 g)
1 (15 ounce) can whole kernel corn with liquid	425 g

- Cut large pieces of stew meat in half and brown in large skillet.

- In 4 or 5-quart (4 L) slow cooker, combine stew meat, tomatoes, taco seasoning mix, beans, corn and ¾ cup (180 ml) water. (If you are not into "spicy", use original recipe stewed tomatoes instead of Mexican.)

- Cover and cook on LOW for 5 to 7 hours. Serves 6 to 8.

TIP: For garnish top each serving with chopped green onions.

Spicy Sausage Soup

1 pound mild bulk sausage	.5 kg
1 pound hot bulk sausage	.5 kg
2 (15 ounce) cans Mexican stewed tomatoes	2 (425 g)
3 cups chopped celery	710 ml
1 cup sliced carrots	240 ml
1 (15 ounce) can cut green beans, drained	425 g
1 (14 ounce) can chicken broth	396 g
1 teaspoon seasoned salt	5 ml

- Combine mild and hot sausage, shape into small balls and place in non-stick skillet. Brown thoroughly and drain.

- Place in large, sprayed slow cooker.

- Add remaining ingredients plus 1 cup (240 ml) water and stir gently so meatballs will not break-up.

- Cover and cook on LOW 6 to 7 hours. Serves 6 to 8.

Tortilla Soup

3 large boneless, skinless chicken breast halves, cubed	
1 (10 ounce) package frozen whole kernel corn, thawed	**280 g**
1 onion, chopped	
3 (14 ounce) cans chicken broth	**3 (396 g)**
1 (6 ounce) can tomato paste	**168 g**
2 (10 ounce) cans tomatoes and green chilies	**2 (280 g)**
2 teaspoons ground cumin	**10 ml**
1 teaspoon chili powder	**5 ml**
1 teaspoon minced garlic	**5 ml**
6 corn tortillas	

- In large slow cooker, combine chicken cubes, corn, onion, broth, tomato paste, tomatoes and green chilies, cumin, chili powder, 1 teaspoon (5 ml) salt and garlic.

- Cover and cook on LOW for 5 to 7 hours or on HIGH for 3 hours to 3 hours 30 minutes.

- While soup is cooking, cut tortillas into ¼-inch (.6 cm) strips and place on baking sheet.

- Bake at 375° (190° C) for about 5 minutes or until crisp.

- Serve baked tortilla strips with soup. Serves 6 to 8.

Southern Soup

1½ cups dried black-eyed peas	360 ml
2 - 3 cups cooked, cubed ham	480 ml
1 (15 ounce) can whole kernel corn	425 g
1 (10 ounce) package frozen cut okra, thawed	280 g
1 onion, chopped	
1 large potato, cut into small cubes	
2 teaspoons Cajun seasoning	10 ml
1 (14 ounce) can chicken broth	396 g
2 (15 ounce) cans Mexican stewed tomatoes	2 (425 g)

- Rinse peas and drain. In large saucepan, combine peas and 5 cups (1.3 L) water.

- Bring to a boil, reduce heat, simmer about 10 minutes and drain.

- In 5 or 6-quart (5 L) slow cooker, combine peas, ham, corn, okra, onion, potato, seasoning, broth and 2 cups (480 ml) water.

- Cover and cook on LOW for 6 to 8 hours.

- Add stewed tomatoes and continue cooking for additional 1 hour. Serves 6 to 8.

Saucy Cabbage Soup

1 pound lean ground beef	.5 kg
1 small head cabbage, chopped	
2 (15 ounce) cans jalapeno pinto beans with liquid	2 (425 g)
1 (15 ounce) can tomato sauce	425 g
1 (15 ounce) can Mexican stewed tomatoes	425 g
1 (14 ounce) can beef broth	396 g
2 teaspoons ground cumin	10 ml

- In skillet brown ground beef, drain and place in 5 to 6-quart (5 L) slow cooker.

- Add cabbage, beans, tomato sauce, tomatoes, broth, cumin and 1 cup (240 ml) water and mix well.

- Cover and cook on LOW for 5 to 6 hours or until cabbage is tender. Serves 4 to 6.

Soup with a Zip

2 (15 ounce) cans Mexican stewed tomatoes	2 (425 g)
2 (14 ounce) cans chicken broth	2 (396 g)
2 (10 ounce) cans chicken noodle soup	2 (280 g)
1 (15 ounce) can shoe-peg corn, drained	425 g
1 (15 ounce) can cut green beans, drained	425 g
Shredded pepper-Jack cheese	

- Place all ingredients except cheese in 4 to 5-quart (4 L) slow cooker and mix well.

- Cover and cook on LOW for 2 to 3 hours. When ready to serve, sprinkle shredded cheese over each bowl of soup. Serves 4 to 6.

Potato and Leek Soup

1 (1 ounce) packet white sauce mix	28 g
1 (28 ounce) package frozen hashbrown potatoes with onions and peppers	794 g
3 medium leeks, sliced	
3 cups cooked, cubed ham	710 ml
1 (12 ounce) can evaporated milk	340 g
1 (8 ounce) carton sour cream	227 g

- In 4 to 5-quart (4 L) slow cooker, pour 3 cups (710 ml) water and stir white sauce until smooth.

- Add hashbrown potatoes, leeks, ham and evaporated milk.

- Cover and cook on LOW for 7 to 9 hours or on HIGH for 3 hours 30 minutes to 4 hours 30 minutes.

- When ready to serve, turn heat to HIGH. Take out about 2 cups (480 ml) hot soup and pour into separate bowl. Stir in sour cream and return to cooker.

- Cover and continue cooking for 15 minutes or until mixture is thoroughly hot. Serves 6 to 8.

Pork and Hominy Soup

2 pounds pork shoulder	1 kg
1 onion, chopped	
2 ribs celery, sliced	
2 (15 ounce) cans yellow hominy with liquid	2 (425 g)
2 (15 ounce) cans stewed tomatoes	2 (425 g)
2 (14 ounce) cans chicken broth	2 (396 g)
1½ teaspoons ground cumin	7 ml

- Cut pork into ½-inch (1.2 cm) cubes.

- Sprinkle pork cubes with a little salt and pepper and brown in skillet.

- Place in 5 to 6-quart (5 L) slow cooker.

- Combine onion, celery, hominy, stewed tomatoes, cumin and 1 cup (240 ml) water.

- Pour over pork cubes.

- Cover and cook on HIGH for 6 to 7 hours.

- Serve with warmed, buttered tortillas and top each bowl of soup with some shredded cheese and chopped green onions. Serves 6 to 8.

Pizza Soup

3 (10 ounce) cans tomato-bisque soup	3 (280 g)
1 (10 ounce) can French onion soup	280 g
2 teaspoons Italian seasoning	10 ml
¾ cup tiny pasta shells	180 ml
1½ cups shredded mozzarella cheese	360 ml

- In 4 to 6-quart (4 L) slow cooker, place 4 cans soup, Italian seasoning and 1½ soup cans water. Turn heat setting to HIGH and cook 1 hour or until mixture is hot.

- Add pasta shells or ditali and cook for 1½ to 2 hours or until pasta is cooked. Stir several times to keep pasta from sticking to bottom of slow cooker.

- Turn heat off, add mozzarella cheese and stir until cheese melts. Serves 6 to 8.

TIP: For a special way to serve this soup, sprinkle some french fried onions over top of each serving.

Pinto Bean-Vegetable Soup

4 (15 ounce) cans seasoned pinto beans with liquid	4 (425 g)
1 (10 ounce) package frozen Seasoning Blend	
chopped onions and peppers	280 g
2 cups chopped celery	480 ml
2 (14 ounce) cans chicken broth	2 (396 g)
1 teaspoon Cajun seasoning	5 ml
⅛ teaspoon cayenne pepper	.5 ml

- Place all ingredients plus 1 cup (240 ml) water in 5-quart (5 L) slow cooker and stir well.

- Cover and cook on LOW 5 to 6 hours. Serves 6 to 8.

Pasta-Veggie Soup

2 yellow squash, peeled, chopped	
2 zucchini, sliced	
1 (10 ounce) package frozen whole kernel corn, thawed	280 g
1 sweet red bell pepper, chopped	
1 (15 ounce) can stewed tomatoes	425 g
1 teaspoon Italian seasoning	5 ml
2 teaspoons dried oregano	10 ml
2 (14 ounce) cans beef broth	2 (396 g)
¾ cup small shell pasta	180 ml

- In 6-quart (6 L) slow cooker, combine squash, zucchini, corn, bell pepper, tomatoes, seasonings, beef broth and 2 cups (480 ml) water.

- Cover and cook on LOW for 6 to 7 hours.

- Add pasta shells and cook and additional 30 to 45 minutes or until pasta is tender.

- Garnish with a sprinkle of shredded mozzarella cheese on each bowl of soup. Serves 4 to 5.

Navy Bean Soup

8 slices thick-cut bacon, divided
1 carrot
3 (15 ounce) cans navy beans with liquid   **3 (425 g)**
3 ribs celery, chopped
1 onion, chopped
2 (15 ounce) cans chicken broth   **2 (425 g)**
1 teaspoon Italian herb seasoning   **5 ml**
1 (10 ounce) can cream of chicken soup   **280 g**

- Cook bacon in skillet, drain and crumble. (Reserve 2 crumbled slices for garnish.)

- Cut carrot in half lengthwise and slice.

- In 5 to 6-quart (5 L) slow cooker, combine most of crumbled bacon, carrot, beans, celery, onion, broth, seasoning, 1 cup (240 ml) water and stir to mix.

- Cover and cook on LOW for 5 to 6 hours.

- Ladle 2 cups (480 ml) soup mixture into food processor or blender and process until smooth.

- Return to cooker, add cream of chicken soup and stir to mix.

- Turn heat to HIGH and cook additional 10 to 15 minutes. Serves 6 to 8.

Meatball Soup

1 (32 ounce) package frozen meatballs	1 kg
2 (15 ounce) cans stewed tomatoes	2 (425 g)
3 large potatoes, peeled, diced	
4 carrots, peeled, sliced	
2 medium onions, chopped	
2 (14 ounce) cans beef broth	2 (396 g)
2 tablespoons cornstarch	30 ml

- In sprayed 6-quart (6 L) slow cooker combine meatballs, tomatoes, potatoes, carrots, onions, beef broth, a little salt and pepper and 1 cup (240 ml) water.

- Cover and cook on LOW for 5 to 6 hours.

- Turn heat to HIGH and combine cornstarch with ¼ cup (60 ml) water. Pour into cooker and cook additional 10 or 15 minutes or until slightly thick. Serves 4 to 6.

Italian Bean Soup

2 (15 ounce) cans great northern beans with liquid	**2 (425 g)**
2 (15 ounce) cans pinto beans with liquid	**2 (425 g)**
1 large onion, chopped	
1 tablespoon instant beef bouillon granules	**15 ml**
1 tablespoon minced garlic	**15 ml**
2 teaspoons Italian seasoning	**10 ml**
2 (15 ounce) cans Italian stewed tomatoes	**2 (425 g)**
1 (15 ounce) can cut green beans, drained	**425 g**

- In large slow cooker, combine both cans of beans, onion, beef bouillon, garlic, Italian seasoning and 2 cups (240 ml) water.

- Cover and cook on LOW for 6 to 8 hours.

- Turn heat to HIGH, add stewed tomatoes and green beans and stir well.

- Continue cooking for additional 30 minutes or until green beans are tender. Serves 6 to 8.

TIP: Serve with crispy Italian toast.

Hamburger Soup

2 pounds lean ground beef	1 kg
2 (15 ounce) cans chili without beans	2 (425 g)
1 (16 ounce) package frozen mixed vegetables, thawed	.5 kg
3 (14 ounce) cans beef broth	3 (396 g)
2 (15 ounce) cans stewed tomatoes	2 (425 g)
1 teaspoon seasoned salt	5 ml

- In skillet, brown ground beef until no longer pink.

- Place in 6-quart (6 L) slow cooker.

- Add chili, vegetables, broth, tomatoes, 1 cup (240 ml) water and seasoned salt and stir well.

- Cover and cook on LOW for 6 to 7 hours. Serves 6 to 8.

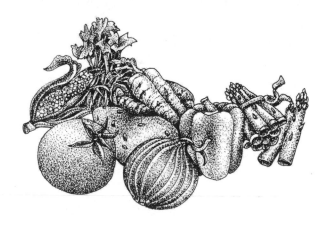

Ham, Bean and Pasta Soup

1 onion, finely chopped	
2 ribs celery, chopped	
2 teaspoons minced garlic	10 ml
2 (14 ounce) cans chicken broth	2 (396 g)
2 (15 ounce) cans pork and beans with liquid	2 (425 g)
3 cups cooked, cubed ham	710 ml
⅓ cup pasta shells	80 ml

- In 5 or 6-quart (5 L) slow cooker combine onion, celery, garlic, chicken broth, beans, ham and 1 cup (240 ml) water.

- Cover and cook on LOW for 4 to 5 hours.

- Turn cooker to HIGH heat, add pasta and cook additional 35 to 45 minutes or until pasta is tender.

- Garnish each serving with cooked, crisp and crumbled bacon. Serves 6 to 8.

French Onion Soup

5 - 6 sweet onions, thinly sliced	
1 clove garlic, minced	
2 tablespoons butter	30 ml
2 (14 ounce) cans beef broth	2 (425 g)
2 teaspoons Worcestershire sauce	10 ml
6 - 8 (1 inch) slices French bread	6 - 8
	(2.5 cm)
8 slices Swiss cheese	

- In large skillet, cook onions on low heat (DO NOT BROWN) in hot butter for about 20 minutes and stir several times.

- Transfer onion mixture to 4 to 5-quart (4 L) slow cooker. Add beef broth, Worcestershire and 1 cup (240 ml) water.

- Cover and cook on LOW for 5 to 8 hours or on HIGH for 2 hours 30 minutes to 4 hours.

- Before serving soup, toast bread slices with cheese slice on top. Broil for 3 to 4 minutes or until cheese is light brown and bubbly.

- Ladle soup into bowls and top with toast. Serves 6 to 8.

Tortellini Soup

1 (1 ounce) packet white sauce mix	28 g
3 boneless, skinless chicken breast halves	
1 (14 ounce) can chicken broth	396 g
1 teaspoon minced garlic	5 ml
½ teaspoon dried basil	2 ml
½ teaspoon oregano	2 ml
½ teaspoon cayenne pepper	2 ml
1 (8 ounce) package cheese tortellini	227 g
1½ cups half-and-half cream	360 ml
6 cups fresh baby spinach	1.5 L

- Place white sauce mix in sprayed 5 to 6-quart (5 L) slow cooker.

- Stir in 4 cups (1 L) water and stir gradually until mixture is smooth.

- Cut chicken into 1-inch (2.5 cm) pieces. Add chicken, broth, garlic, basil, oregano, red pepper and ½ teaspoon (2 ml) salt to mixture.

- Cover and cook on LOW for 6 to 7 hours or on HIGH for 3 hours.

- Stir in tortellini, cover and cook 1 hour more on HIGH.

- Stir in cream and fresh spinach and cook just enough for soup to get hot. Serves 4 to 6.

TIP: Sprinkle a little shredded parmesan cheese on top of each serving.

Enchilada Soup

1 pound lean ground beef, browned, drained	.5 kg
1 (15 ounce) can Mexican stewed tomatoes	425 g
1 (15 ounce) can pinto beans with liquid	425 g
1 (15 ounce) can whole kernel corn with liquid	425 g
1 onion, chopped	
2 (10 ounce) cans enchilada sauce	2 (280 g)
1 (8 ounce) package shredded 4-cheese blend	227 g

- Spray 5 to 6-quart (5 L) slow cooker.

- Combine beef, tomatoes, beans, corn, onion, enchilada sauce and 1 cup (240 ml) water and mix well.

- Cover and cook on LOW for 6 to 8 hours or on HIGH for 3 to 4 hours.

- Stir in shredded cheese.

- If desired, top each serving with a few crushed tortilla chips. Serves 6 to 8.

Delicious Broccoli-Cheese Soup

1 (16 ounce) package frozen chopped broccoli, thawed	.5 kg
1 (12 ounce) package cubed Velveeta® cheese	340 g
1 (2 ounce) packet white sauce mix	57 g
1 (1 ounce) packet dry vegetable soup mix	28 g
1 (12 ounce) can evaporated milk	340 g
1 (14 ounce) can chicken broth	396 g

• In large sprayed, slow cooker, combine all ingredients plus 2 cups (480 ml) water and stir well.

• Cover and cook on LOW for 6 to 7 hours or on HIGH for 3 hours 30 minutes to 4 hours.

• Stir for 1 hour before serving time. Serves 4 to 6.

Tasty Black Bean Soup

1 pound hot sausage	.5 kg
1 onion, chopped	
2 (14 ounce) cans chicken broth	2 (396 g)
2 (15 ounce) cans Mexican stewed tomatoes	2 (425 g)
1 green bell pepper, chopped	
2 (15 ounce) cans black beans, rinsed, drained	2 (425 g)

• In large skillet, break up sausage and brown with onion. Drain off fat and place in large slow cooker.

• Add chicken broth, stewed tomatoes, bell pepper, black beans and 1 cup (240 ml) water. Cover and cook on LOW for 3 to 5 hours. Serves 4 to 6.

Sausage-Pizza Soup

1 (16 ounce) package Italian link sausage, thinly sliced	.5 kg
1 onion, chopped	
2 (4 ounce) cans sliced mushrooms	2 (114 g)
1 small green bell pepper, cored, seeded, julienned	
1 (15 ounce) can Italian stewed tomatoes	425 g
1 (14 ounce) can beef broth	396 g
1 (8 ounce) can pizza sauce	227 g
Shredded mozzarella cheese	

- Combine all ingredients in slow cooker and stir well.

- Cover and cook on LOW for 4 to 5 hours.

- Sprinkle mozzarella cheese over each serving. Serves 4 to 6.

Creamy Vegetable Soup

3 (14 ounce) cans chicken broth	3 (396 g)
¼ cup (½ stick) butter, melted	60 ml
1 (16 ounce) package frozen mixed vegetables	.5 kg
1 onion, chopped	
3 ribs celery, sliced	
1 teaspoon ground cumin	5 ml
3 zucchini, coarsely chopped	
2 cups chopped, fresh broccoli	480 ml
1 cup half-and-half cream	240 ml

- In large slow cooker, combine broth, butter, vegetables, onion, celery, cumin, 1 teaspoon (5 ml) each of salt and pepper and stir well.

- Cover and cook on LOW for 6 to 7 hours or on HIGH for 3 to 4 hours.

- Stir in zucchini and broccoli. If not using HIGH temperature, turn heat to HIGH and cook additional 30 minutes to 1 hour or until broccoli is tender-crisp.

- Turn off heat and stir in half-and-half cream. Let stand 10 minutes before serving. Serves 6 to 8.

Cream of Zucchini Soup

1 small onion, very finely chopped	
3½ - 4 cups grated zucchini with peel	830 ml
2 (14 ounce) cans chicken broth	2 (396 g)
1 teaspoon seasoned salt	5 ml
1 teaspoon dried dill weed	5 ml
½ teaspoon white pepper	2 ml
2 tablespoons butter, melted	30 ml
1 (8 ounce) carton sour cream	227 g

- In small, sprayed slow cooker, combine all ingredients except sour cream.

- Cover and cook on LOW for 2 hours.

- Fold in sour cream and continue cooking for about 10 minutes or just until soup is hot. Serves 4.

Black Bean Soup

2 (14 ounce) cans chicken broth	2 (396 g)
3 (15 ounce) cans black beans, rinsed, drained	3 (425 g)
2 (10 ounce) cans tomatoes and green chilies	2 (280 g)
1 onion, chopped	
1 teaspoon ground cumin	5 ml
½ teaspoon dried thyme	2 ml
½ teaspoon dried oregano	2 ml
2 - 3 cups cooked, finely diced ham	480 ml

- In slow cooker, combine chicken broth and black beans and turn cooker to HIGH.

- Cook just long enough for ingredients to get hot.

- With potato masher, mash about half of the beans in cooker.

- Reduce heat to LOW and add tomatoes and green chilies, onion, spices, diced ham and ¾ cup (180 ml) water.

- Cover and cook for 5 to 6 hours. Serves 6 to 8.

Confetti-Chicken Soup

1 pound boneless, skinless chicken thighs	.5 kg
1 (6.2 ounce) package chicken and herb-flavored rice	168 g
3 (14 ounce) cans chicken broth	3 (396 g)
3 carrots, sliced	
1 (10 ounce) can cream of chicken soup	280 g
1½ tablespoons chicken seasoning	22 ml
1 (10 ounce) package frozen whole kernel corn, thawed	280 g
1 (10 ounce) package frozen baby green peas, thawed	280 g

- Cut thighs in thin strips.

- In 5 or 6-quart (5 L) slow cooker, combine chicken, rice, chicken broth, carrots and 1 cup (240 ml) water.

- Cover and cook on LOW for 8 to 9 hours.

- About 30 minutes before serving, turn heat to HIGH and add corn and peas to cooker. Continue cooking for additional 30 minutes. Serves 4 to 6.

Turkey and Mushroom Soup

Another great way to use leftover chicken or turkey

2 cups sliced shitake mushrooms	480 ml
2 ribs celery, sliced	
1 small onion, chopped	
2 tablespoons butter	30 ml
1 (15 ounce) can sliced carrots	425 g
2 (14 ounce) cans chicken broth	396 g
½ cup orzo pasta	120 ml
2 cups cooked, chopped turkey or chicken	480 ml

- In skillet, saute mushrooms, celery and onion in butter.

- Transfer vegetables to slow cooker and add carrots, broth, orzo and turkey. (Do not use smoked turkey.)

- Cover and cook on LOW for 2 to 3 hours or on HIGH for 1 to 2 hours. Serves 4 to 6.

Tasty Cabbage and Beef Soup

1 pound lean ground beef	.5 kg
1 (16 ounce) package coleslaw mix	.5 kg
1 (15 ounce) can cut green beans	425 g
1 (15 ounce) can whole kernel corn	425 g
2 (15 ounce) cans Italian stewed tomatoes	2 (425 g)
2 (14 ounce) cans beef broth	2 (396 g)

- In skillet, brown ground beef, drain fat and place in large slow cooker.

- Add slaw mix, green beans, corn, tomatoes and beef broth and add a little salt and pepper.

- Cover and cook on LOW for 7 to 9 hours. Serve with cornbread. Serves 6 to 8.

Chili Soup

3 (15 ounce) cans chili with beans	3 (425 g)
1 (15 ounce) can whole kernel corn	425 g
1 (14 ounce) can beef broth	396 g
2 (15 ounce) cans Mexican stewed tomatoes	2 (425 g)
2 teaspoons ground cumin	10 ml
2 teaspoons chili powder	10 ml

- In 5 to 6-quart (5 L) slow cooker, combine chili, corn, broth, tomatoes, cumin, chili powder and 1 cup (240 ml) water.

- Cover and cook on LOW for 4 to 5 hours. Serve with warm, buttered flour tortillas. Serves 6 to 8.

Chicken-Pasta Soup

1½ pounds boneless, skinless chicken thighs, cubed	.7 kg
1 onion, chopped	
3 carrots, sliced	
½ cup halved, pitted ripe olives	120 ml
1 teaspoon minced garlic	5 ml
3 (14 ounce) cans chicken broth	3 (396 g)
1 (15 ounce) can Italian stewed tomatoes	425 g
1 teaspoon Italian seasoning	5 ml
½ cup small shell pasta	120 ml
Parmesan cheese	

- In slow cooker, combine all ingredients except shell pasta and parmesan cheese. Cover and cook on LOW for 8 to 9 hours.
  About 30 minutes before serving, add pasta and stir.

- Increase heat to HIGH and cook additional 20 to 30 minutes. Garnish with parmesan cheese.
  Serves 6 to 8.

Chicken and Rice Soup

1 (6 ounce) package long grain wild rice mix	1 (180 g)
1 (1.3 ounce) envelope chicken noodle soup mix	1 (32 g)
2 (10 ounce) cans cream of chicken soup	2 (284 g)
2 ribs celery, chopped	2
1 to 2 cups cubed, cooked chicken	250 to 500 mL

- In 5 to 6-quart (6 L) slow cooker, combine rice mix, noodle soup mix, chicken soup, celery, cubed chicken and about 6 cups (1.75 L) water.

- Cover and cook on LOW for 2 to 3 hours.
  Serves 4 to 6.

Chicken and Barley Soup

1½ - 2 pounds boneless, skinless chicken thighs	.7 kg
1 (16 ounce) package frozen stew vegetables	.5 kg
1 (1 ounce) packet dry vegetable soup mix	28 g
1¼ cups pearl barley	300 ml
2 (14 ounce) cans chicken broth	2 (396 g)
1 teaspoon white pepper	5 ml

- Spray large slow cooker, combine all ingredients with 1 teaspoon (5 ml) salt and 4 cups (1 L) water.

- Cover and cook on LOW for 5 to 6 hours or on HIGH for 3 hours. Serves 6 to 8.

Vegetable-Lentil Soup

2 (19 ounce) cans lentil home-style soup	2 (538 g)
1 (15 ounce) can stewed tomatoes	425 g
1 (14 ounce) can chicken broth	396 g
1 onion, chopped	
1 green bell pepper, chopped	
3 ribs celery, sliced	
1 carrot, halved lengthwise, sliced	
2 teaspoons minced garlic	10 ml
1 teaspoon dried marjoram leaves	5 ml

- Combine all ingredients in slow cooker and stir well.

- Cover and cook on LOW for 5 to 6 hours.
  Serves 6 to 8.

Turkey-Tortilla Soup
This is great for leftover turkey.

2 (14 ounce) cans chicken broth	2 (396 g)
2 (15 ounce) cans Mexican stewed tomatoes	2 (425 g)
1 (16 ounce) package frozen succotash, thawed	.5 kg
2 teaspoons chili powder	10 ml
1 teaspoon dried cilantro	5 ml
2 cups crushed tortilla chips, divided	480 ml
2½ cups cooked, chopped leftover turkey	600 ml

- In large slow cooker, combine broth, tomatoes, succotash, chili powder, cilantro, ⅓ cup (80 ml) crushed tortilla chips and turkey or chicken and stir well.

- Cover and cook on LOW for 3 to 5 hours.

- When ready to serve, sprinkle remaining chips over each serving. Serves 6 to 8.

TIP: Do not use smoked turkey.

Cheesy Potato Soup

6 medium potatoes, peeled, cubed	
1 onion, very finely chopped	
2 (14 ounce) cans chicken broth	2 (396 g)
½ teaspoon white pepper	2 ml
1 (8 ounce) package shredded American cheese	227 g
1 cup half-and-half cream	240 ml

- In slow cooker, combine potatoes, onion, chicken broth and white pepper.

- Cover and cook on LOW for 8 to 10 hours. With potato masher, mash potatoes in slow cooker.

- About 1 hour before serving, stir in cheese and cream and cook additional 1 hour. Serves 4 to 6.

Cheddar Soup Plus

2 cups milk	**480 ml**
1 (7 ounce) package cheddar-broccoli soup starter	**198 g**
1 cup cooked, finely chopped chicken breasts	**240 ml**
1 (10 ounce) frozen green peas, thawed	**280 g**
Shredded cheddar cheese	

- Place 5 cups (1.3 L) water and 2 cups (480 ml) milk in slow cooker. Set heat on HIGH until water and milk come to a boil.

- Stir contents of soup starter into hot water and milk and stir well. Add chopped chicken, green peas and a little salt and pepper.

- Cook on LOW for 2 to 3 hours.

- To serve, sprinkle cheddar cheese over each serving of soup. Serves 4.

Cajun Bean Soup

1 (20 ounce) package Cajun-flavored, 16-bean soup mix with flavor packet	567 g
2 cups cooked, finely chopped ham	480 ml
1 chopped onion	
2 (15 ounce) cans stewed tomatoes	2 (425 g)

- Soak beans overnight in large slow cooker. After soaking, drain water and cover with 2 inches water over beans.

- Cover and cook on LOW for 5 to 6 hours or until beans are tender.

- Add ham, onion, stewed tomatoes and flavor packet in bean soup mix.

- Cook on HIGH for 30 to 45 minutes.

- Serve with cornbread. Serves 4 to 6.

Black-Eyed Pea Soup

5 slices thick-cut bacon, diced
1 onion, chopped
1 green bell pepper, chopped
3 ribs celery, sliced
3 (15 ounce) cans jalapeno black-eyed peas
   with liquid   3 (425 g)
2 (15 ounce) cans stewed tomatoes with liquid   2 (425 g)
1 teaspoon chicken seasoning   5 ml

- In skillet, cook bacon pieces until crisp, drain on paper towel and put in slow cooker.

- With bacon drippings in skillet, saute onion and bell peppers, but do not brown.

- To bacon in slow cooker, add onions, bell pepper, celery, black-eyed peas, stewed tomatoes, 1½ cups (360 ml) water, 1 teaspoon (5 ml) salt and chicken seasoning.

- Cover and cook on LOW for 3 to 4 hours. Serves 6 to 8.

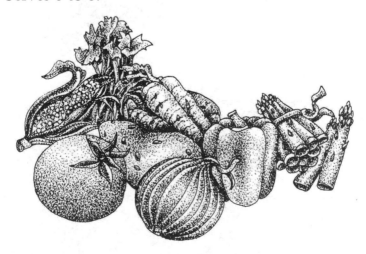

Beefy Rice Soup

1 pound lean beef stew meat	.5 kg
1 (14 ounce) can beef broth	396 g
1 (7 ounce) box beef-flavored rice and vermicelli mix	198 g
1 (10 ounce) package frozen peas and carrots	280 g
2½ cups vegetable juice	600 ml

- Sprinkle stew meat with seasoned pepper, brown in non-stick skillet, drain and place in large slow cooker.

- Add broth, rice and vermicelli mix, peas, carrots, vegetable juice and 2 cups (480 ml) water.

- Cover and cook on LOW for 6 to 7 hours. Serves 4 to 6.

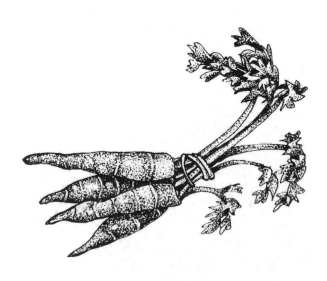

Beef and Black Bean Soup

1 pound lean ground beef	**.5 kg**
2 onions, chopped	
2 cups sliced celery	**480 ml**
2 (14 ounce) cans beef broth	**2 (396 g)**
1 (15 ounce) can Mexican stewed tomatoes	**425 g**
2 (15 ounce) cans black beans, rinsed, drained	**2 (425 g)**

- In skillet, brown beef until no longer pink. Place in 5 to 6-quart (5 L) slow cooker.

- Add onions, celery, broth, tomatoes, black beans, ¾ cup (180 ml) water plus a little salt and pepper.

- Cover and cook on LOW for 6 to 7 hours or on HIGH for 3 hours to 3 hours 30 minutes. Serves 6 to 8.

TIP: If you like a zestier soup, add 1 teaspoon (5 ml) chili powder.

Beef and Noodle Soup

1½ pounds lean ground beef	.7 kg
1 onion, chopped	
2 (15 ounce) cans mixed vegetables, drained	2 (425 g)
2 (15 ounce) cans Italian stewed tomatoes	2 (425 g)
2 (14 ounce) cans beef broth	2 (396 g)
1 teaspoon dried oregano	5 ml
1 cup medium egg noodles	240 ml

- In skillet, brown and cook ground beef until no longer pink and transfer to slow cooker. Add onion, mixed vegetables, stewed tomatoes, beef broth and oregano.

- Cover and cook on LOW for 4 to 5 hours.

- In saucepan, cook noodles according to package direction.

- Add noodles to slow cooker and cook 30 minutes. Serves 4 to 6.

Beef and Noodle Soup

1½ pounds lean ground beef	.7 kg
1 onion, chopped	
2 (15 ounce) cans mixed vegetables, drained	2 (425 g)
2 (15 ounce) cans Italian stewed tomatoes	2 (425 g)
2 (14 ounce) cans beef broth	2 (396 g)
1 teaspoon dried oregano	5 ml
1 cup medium egg noodles	240 ml

- In skillet, brown and cook ground beef until no longer pink and transfer to slow cooker. Add onion, mixed vegetables, stewed tomatoes, beef broth and oregano.

- Cover and cook on LOW for 4 to 5 hours.

- In saucepan, cook noodles according to package direction. Add noodles to slow cooker and cook 30 minutes. Serves 4 to 6.

Beans 'N' Sausage Soup

1 pound hot Italian sausage	.5 kg
1 onion, chopped	
1 (15 ounce) can Italian stewed tomatoes	425 g
2 (5 ounce) cans black beans, rinsed, drained	2 (143 g)
2 (15 ounce) cans navy beans with liquid	2 (425 g)
2 (14 ounce) cans beef broth	2 (396 g)
1 teaspoon minced garlic	5 ml
1 teaspoon dried basil	5 ml

- Cut sausage into ½-inch (1.2 cm) pieces. In skillet, brown sausage and onion, drain and transfer to 5 to 6-quart (5 L) slow cooker.

- Stir in tomatoes, black beans, navy beans, broth, garlic and basil and mix well. Cover and cook on LOW for 5 to 7 hours. Serves 6 to 8.

Beans and Barley Soup

2 (15 ounce) cans pinto beans with liquid	2 (425 g)
3 (14 ounce) cans chicken broth	3 (396 g)
½ cup quick-cooking barley	120 ml
1 (15 ounce) can Italian stewed tomatoes	425 g

- In 6-quart (6 L) slow cooker, combine beans, broth, barley, stewed tomatoes and ½ teaspoon (2 ml) pepper and stir well.

- Cover and cook on LOW for 4 to 5 hours. Serves 6 to 8.

Minestrone Soup

2 (15 ounce) cans Italian stewed tomatoes	2 (425 g)
2 (16 ounce) packages frozen vegetables and pasta seasoned sauce	2 (.5 kg)
3 (14 ounce) cans beef broth	3 (396 g)
2 ribs celery, chopped	
2 potatoes, peeled, cubed	
1 teaspoon Italian herb seasoning	5 ml
2 (15 ounce) cans kidney beans, drained, rinsed	2 (425 g)
2 teaspoons minced garlic	10 ml

- In large sprayed slow cooker, combine tomatoes, vegetables, broth, celery, potatoes, seasoning, beans, garlic and 1 cup (240 ml) water and mix well.

- Cover and cook on LOW for 4 to 6 hours. Serves 6 to 8.

Winter Minestrone

1 pound Italian sausage links	.5 kg
2½ cups butternut or acorn squash	600 ml
2 medium potatoes, peeled	
2 medium fennel bulbs, trimmed	
1 onion, chopped	
1 (15 ounce) can kidney beans, rinsed, drained	425 g
2 teaspoons minced garlic	10 ml
1 teaspoon Italian seasoning	5 ml
2 (14 ounce) cans chicken broth	2 (396 g)
1 cup dry white wine	240 ml
3 - 4 cups fresh spinach	710 ml

- Cut sausage, potatoes and fennel into ½-inch (1.2 cm) slices.

- In skillet cook sausage until brown and drain.

- In large slow cooker, combine squash, potatoes, fennel, onion, beans, garlic and Italian seasoning.

- Top with sausage and pour chicken broth and wine over all.

- Cover and cook on LOW for 7 to 9 hours.

- Stir in spinach, cover and cook additional 10 minutes. Serves 6 to 8.

Pancho Villa Stew

3 cups cooked, diced ham	710 ml
1 pound smoked sausage	.5 kg
3 (14 ounce) cans chicken broth	3 (396 g)
1 (15 ounce) can diced tomatoes	425 g
1 (7 ounce) can chopped green chilies	198 g
1 onion, chopped	
2 (15 ounce) cans pinto beans with liquid	2 (425 g)
1 (15 ounce) can whole kernel corn	425 g
1 teaspoon garlic powder	5 ml
2 teaspoons ground cumin	10 ml
2 teaspoons cocoa	10 ml
1 teaspoon dried oregano	5 ml

- Cut sausage into ½-inch (1.2 cm) pieces.

- In slow cooker, combine all ingredients and 1 teaspoon (5 ml) salt and stir well.

- Cover and cook on LOW for 5 to 7 hours.

- Serve with buttered, flour tortillas. Serves 6 to 8.

Chicken-Tortellini Stew

1 (9 ounce) package cheese-filled tortellini	255 g
2 medium yellow squash, halved, sliced	
1 sweet red bell pepper, coarsely chopped	
1 onion, chopped	
2 (14 ounce) cans chicken broth	2 (396 g)
1 teaspoon dried rosemary	5 ml
½ teaspoon dried basil	2 ml
2 cups cooked, chopped chicken	480 ml

- Place tortellini, squash, bell pepper and onion in slow cooker. Stir in broth, rosemary, basil and chicken.

- Cover and cook on LOW for 2 to 4 hours or until tortellini and vegetables are tender. Serves 4.

A Different Stew

2 pounds premium lean beef stew meat	1 kg
1 (16 ounce) package frozen Oriental stir-fry vegetables, thawed	.5 kg
1 (10 ounce) can beefy mushroom soup	280 g
1 (10 ounce) can beef broth	280 g
⅔ cup bottled sweet-and-sour sauce	160 ml
1 tablespoon beef seasoning	15 ml

- In skillet brown stew meat sprinkled with ½ teaspoon (2 ml) black pepper and place in slow cooker.

- In bowl, combine vegetables, soup, broth, sweet-and-sour sauce, beef seasoning and 1 cup (240 ml) water. Pour over stew meat and stir well.

- Cover and cook on LOW for 5 to 7 hours. Serves 4 to 6.

Southern Ham Stew
This is great served with cornbread.

2 cups dried black-eyed peas	480 ml
3 cups cooked, cubed ham	710 ml
1 large onion, chopped	
2 cups sliced celery	480 ml
1 (15 ounce) can yellow hominy, drained	425 g
2 (15 ounce) cans stewed tomatoes	2 (425 g)
1 (10 ounce) can chicken broth	280 g
2 teaspoons seasoned salt	10 ml
2 tablespoons cornstarch	30 ml

- Rinse and drain dried black-eyed peas in saucepan. Cover peas with water, bring to a boil and drain again.

- Place peas in large slow cooker and add 5 cups (1.3 L) water, ham, onion, celery, hominy, tomatoes, broth and seasoned salt.

- Cover and cook on LOW for 7 to 9 hours. Mix cornstarch with ⅓ cup (80 ml) water, turn cooker to HIGH heat, pour in cornstarch mixture and stir well.

- Cook just about 10 minutes or until stew thickens. Add good amount of salt and pepper and stir well before serving. Serves 6 to 8.

TIP: If you would like a little spice in the stew, substitute one of the cans of stewed tomatoes with the Mexican stewed tomatoes.

Serious Bean Stew

1 (16 ounce) package smoked sausage links	.5 kg
1 (28 ounce) can baked beans with liquid	794 g
1 (15 ounce) can great northern beans with liquid	425 g
1 (15 ounce) can pinto beans with liquid	425 g
1 (15 ounce) can lentil soup	425 g
1 onion, chopped	
1 teaspoon Cajun seasoning	5 ml
2 (15 ounce) cans stewed tomatoes	2 (425 g)

- Peel skin from sausage links and slice.

- Place in 6-quart (6 L) slow cooker, add remaining ingredients and stir to mix.

- Cover and cook on LOW for 3 to 4 hours.

- Serve with corn muffins. Serves 6 to 8.

Santa Fe Stew
A hearty, filling soup.

1½ pounds lean ground beef	.7 kg
1 (14 ounce) can beef broth	396 g
1 (15 ounce) can whole kernel corn with liquid	425 g
2 (15 ounce) cans pinto beans with liquid	2 (425 g)
2 (15 ounce) cans Mexican stewed tomatoes	2 (425 g)
1 tablespoon beef seasoning	15 ml
1 (16 ounce) package cubed Velveeta® cheese	.5 kg

- In skillet, brown beef until no longer pink.

- Place in 5 to 6-quart (6 L) slow cooker and add broth, corn, beans, tomatoes and beef seasoning.

- Cook on LOW for 5 to 6 hours.

- When ready to serve, fold in cheese and stir until cheese melts. Serves 6 to 8.

TIP: Cornbread is a must to serve with this stew.

Roast and Vegetable Stew

3 cups leftover roast beef, cubed	710 ml
2 (15 ounce) cans stewed tomatoes	2 (425 g)
1 (16 ounce) package frozen mixed vegetables,	
thawed	.5 kg
2 (14 ounce) cans beef broth	2 (396 g)
1 cup cauliflower florets, optional	240 ml
1 cup broccoli florets, optional	240 ml

- Combine all ingredients except cauliflower and broccoli in 6-quart (6 L) slow cooker. Add a little salt and pepper.

- Cover and cook on LOW for 3 to 4 hours.

- Stir in cauliflower and broccoli and continue cooking an additional 2 hours until tender. Serves 6 to 8.

Pork-Vegetable Stew

1 (2 pound) pork tenderloin	1 kg
1 onion, coarsely chopped	
1 sweet red bell pepper, julienned	
1 (16 ounce) package frozen mixed vegetables, thawed	.5 kg
2 tablespoons flour	30 ml
1 (10 ounce) can chicken broth	280 g
½ teaspoon dried rosemary leaves	2 ml
½ teaspoon oregano leaves	2 ml
1 (6 ounce) package long grain-wild rice	168 g

- Cut tenderloin into 1-inch (2.5 cm) cubes. In non-stick skillet, brown tenderloin cubes and place in large, sprayed slow cooker.

- Add onion, bell pepper and mixed vegetables.

- In bowl, stir flour, rosemary and oregano into chicken broth and pour over vegetables.

- Cover and cook on LOW for 4 hours to 4 hours 30 minutes.

- When ready to serve, cook rice according to package directions.

- Serve pork and vegetables over rice. Serves 4 to 6.

Olé! For Stew

1½ - 2 pounds lean beef stew meat	.7 kg
2 (15 ounce) cans pinto beans with liquid	2 (425 g)
1 onion, chopped	
3 carrots, sliced	
2 medium potatoes, cubed	
1 (1 ounce) packet taco seasoning	28 g
2 (15 ounce) cans Mexican stewed tomatoes	2 (425 g)

- Use non-stick skillet to brown stew meat. In large slow cooker, combine meat, pinto beans, onion, carrots, potatoes, taco seasoning and 2 cups (480 ml) water.

- Cover and cook on LOW for 6 to 7 hours. Add stewed tomatoes and cook additional 1 hour. Serves 4 to 6.

TIP: This is great served with warmed, buttered, flour tortillas.

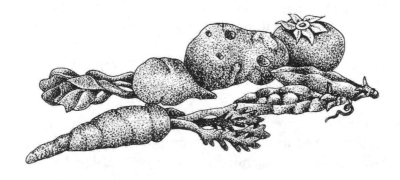

Meatball Stew

1 (18 ounce) package frozen prepared Italian meatballs, thawed	510 g
1 (14 ounce) can beef broth	396 g
1 (15 ounce) can cut green beans	425 g
1 (16 ounce) package baby carrots	.5 kg
2 (15 ounce) cans stewed tomatoes	2 (425 g)
1 tablespoon Worcestershire sauce	15 ml
½ teaspoon ground allspice	2 ml

- Combine all ingredients in slow cooker. Cover and cook on LOW for 3 to 5 hours.
  Serves 4 to 6.

Meatball and Veggie Stew

1 (18 ounce) package frozen cooked meatballs, thawed	510 g
1 (16 ounce) package frozen mixed vegetables	.5 kg
1 (15 ounce) can stewed tomatoes	425 g
1 (12 ounce) jar beef gravy	340 g
2 teaspoons crushed dried basil	10 ml

- Place meatballs and mixed vegetables in 4 to 5-quart (4 L) slow cooker.

- In bowl stir stewed tomatoes, gravy, basil, ½ teaspoon (2 ml) black pepper and ½ cup (120 ml) water. Pour over meatballs and vegetables.

- Cover and cook on LOW for 6 to 7 hours.
  Serves 4 to 6.

Italian-Vegetable Stew

1½ to 2 pounds Italian sausage	.7 kg
2 (16 ounce) packages frozen vegetables	2 (.5 kg)
2 (15 ounce) cans Italian stewed tomatoes	2 (425 g)
1 (14 ounce) can beef broth	396 g
1 teaspoon Italian seasoning	5 ml
½ cup pasta shells	120 ml

- In skillet, brown sausage and cook about 5 minutes and drain.

- In 5 to 6-quart (5 L) slow cooker, combine sausage, vegetables, stewed tomatoes, broth, Italian seasoning and shells and mix well.

- Cover and cook on LOW for 3 to 5 hours. Serves 4 to 6.

Hungarian Stew

2 pounds boneless short ribs	1 kg
1 cup pearl barley	240 ml
1 small onion, chopped	
1 green bell pepper, cored, seeded, chopped	
1 teaspoon minced garlic	5 ml
2 (15 ounce) cans kidney beans, drained	2 (425 g)
2 (14 ounce) cans beef broth	2 (396 g)
1 tablespoon paprika	15 ml

- In slow cooker, combine all ingredients plus 1 cup (240 ml) water.

- Cover and cook on LOW for 8 to 9 hours or on HIGH for 4 hours 30 minutes to 5 hours. Serves 4 to 6.

Hearty Meatball Stew

1 (28 ounce) package frozen meatballs, thawed	794 g
2 (15 ounce) cans Italian stewed tomatoes	2 (425 g)
2 (14 ounce) cans beef broth	2 (396 g)
2 (15 ounce) cans new potatoes	2 (425 g)
1 (16 ounce) package baby carrots	.5 kg
1 tablespoon Step 1 beef seasoning	15 ml

- Place meatballs, stewed tomatoes, beef broth, potatoes, carrots and beef seasoning in 6-quart (6 L) slow cooker.

- Cover and cook on LOW for 6 to 7 hours.

- Serve with corn muffins. Serves 6 to 8.

South-of-the-Border Beef Stew

1½ - 2 pounds boneless, beef chuck roast	**.7 kg**
1 green bell pepper	
2 onions, coarsely chopped	
2 (15 ounce) cans pinto beans with liquid	**2 (425 g)**
½ cup rice	**120 ml**
1 (14 ounce) can beef broth	**396 g**
2 (15 ounce) cans Mexican stewed tomatoes	**2 (425 g)**
1 cup mild or medium green salsa	**240 ml**
2 teaspoons ground cumin	**10 ml**

- Trim fat from beef and cut into 1-inch (2.5 cm) cubes.

- Brown beef in large skillet and place in large, sprayed slow cooker.

- Cut bell pepper into ½-inch (1.2 cm) slices.

- Add remaining ingredients plus 1½ cups (360 ml) water and a little salt.

- Cover and cook on LOW for 7 to 8 hours. Serves 6 to 8.

Ham and Cabbage Stew

2 (15 ounce) can Italian stewed tomatoes	2 (425 g)
3 cups shredded cabbage	710 ml
1 onion, chopped	
1 sweet red bell pepper, cored, seeded , chopped	
2 tablespoons butter, sliced	30 ml
1 (14 ounce) can chicken broth	396 g
¾ teaspoon seasoned salt	4 ml
3 cups cooked, diced ham	710 ml

- In large slow cooker, combine all ingredients and ¾ teaspoons (4 ml) pepper with 1 cup (240 ml) water and stir to mix well.

- Cover and cook on LOW for 5 to 7 hours.

- Serve with cornbread. Serves 4 to 6.

Comfort Stew

1½ pounds select stew meat	.7 kg
2 (10 ounce) cans French onion soup	2 (280 g)
1 (10 ounce) can cream of onion soup	280 g
1 (10 ounce) can cream of celery soup	280 g
1 (16 ounce) package frozen stew vegetables, thawed	.5 kg

- Place stew meat in sprayed slow cooker.

- Add soups as listed and spread evenly over meat. DO NOT STIR. Turn slow cooker to HIGH and cook just long enough for ingredients to get hot.

- Change heat setting to LOW, cover and cook for 7 to 8 hours. Serves 4 to 6.

Chicken Stew Over Biscuits

2 (1 ounce) packets chicken gravy mix	2 (28 g)
2 cups sliced celery	480 ml
1 (10 ounce) package frozen sliced carrots	280 g
1 (10 ounce) package frozen green peas, thawed	280 g
1 teaspoon dried basil	5 ml
3 cups cooked, cubed chicken or turkey	710 ml
Buttermilk biscuits	

- In slow cooker, combine gravy mix, 2 cups (480 ml) water, celery, carrots, peas, basil, ¾ teaspoon (4 ml) each of salt and pepper and chicken.

- Cover and cook on LOW for 6 to 7 hours. Serve over baked refrigerated buttermilk biscuits. Serves 4 to 6.

TIP: If you like thick stew, mix 2 tablespoons (30 ml) cornstarch with ¼ cup (60 ml) water and stir into chicken mixture. Cook additional 30 minutes to thicken.

Chicken Stew

4 large boneless, skinless chicken breast halves, cubed	
3 medium potatoes, peeled, cubed	
1 (26 ounce) jar meatless spaghetti sauce	737 g
1 (15 ounce) can cut green beans, drained	425 g
1 (15 ounce) can whole kernel corn	425 g
1 tablespoon chicken seasoning	15 ml

- Combine cubed chicken, potatoes, spaghetti sauce, green beans, corn, chicken seasoning and ¾ cup (180 ml) water in 5 to 6-quart (5 L) slow cooker.

- Cover and cook on LOW for 6 to 7 hours. Serves 4 to 6.

White Lightning Chili

3 (15 ounce) cans navy beans with liquid	3 (425 g)
3 (14 ounce) cans chicken broth	3 (396 g)
1 (10 ounce) can cream of chicken soup	280 g
2 tablespoons butter, melted	30 ml
2 onions, chopped	
3 cups cooked, chopped chicken or turkey	710 ml
1 (7 ounce) can chopped green chilies	198 g
1 teaspoon minced garlic	5 ml
½ teaspoon dried basil	2 ml
½ teaspoon white pepper	2 ml
⅛ teaspoon cayenne pepper	.5 ml
⅛ teaspoon ground cloves	.5 ml
1 teaspoon ground oregano	5 ml
1 (8 ounce) package shredded 4-cheese blend	227 g

- In slow cooker, combine all ingredients except cheese.

- Cover and cook on LOW for 4 to 5 hours.

- When serving, sprinkle cheese over top of each serving. Serves 6 to 8.

Vegetarian Chili

2 (15 ounce) cans stewed tomatoes	2 (425 g)
1 (15 ounce) can kidney beans, rinsed, drained	425 g
1 (15 ounce) can pinto beans with liquid	425 g
1 onion, chopped	
1 green bell pepper, chopped	
1 tablespoon chili powder	15 ml
1 (7 ounce) package elbow macaroni	198 g
¼ cup (½ stick) butter, sliced	60 ml

- In 4 or 5-quart (4 L) slow cooker, combine tomatoes, kidney beans, pinto beans, onion, bell pepper, chili powder and 1 cup (240 ml) water.

- Cover and cook on LOW for 4 to 5 hours or on HIGH for 2 hours.

- Cook macaroni according to package directions, drain and stir into hot macaroni. Fold into chili.

- If desired, top each serving with shredded cheddar cheese. Serves 4 to 6.

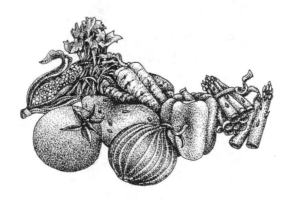

Vegetable Chili

2 (15 ounce) cans navy beans with liquid	2 (425 g)
2 (15 ounce) cans Mexican stewed tomatoes	2 (425 g)
1 (15 ounce) can pinto beans with liquid	425 g
1 (15 ounce) can whole kernel corn	425 g
1 onion, chopped	
3 ribs celery, sliced	
1 tablespoon chili powder	15 ml
2 teaspoons dried oregano leaves	10 ml
1 teaspoon seasoned salt	5 ml

- In 5 to 6-quart (5 L) slow cooker, combine both beans, tomatoes, corn, onion, celery, chili powder, oregano, seasoned salt and 1½ cups (360 ml) water.

- Cover and cook on LOW for 4 to 6 hours.

- Serve with hot, buttered broccoli cornbread. Serves 6 to 8.

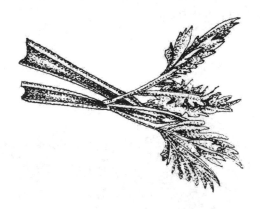

Turkey-Veggie Chili

1 pound ground turkey	.5 kg
2 (15 ounce) cans pinto beans with liquid	2 (425 g)
1 (15 ounce) can great northern beans with liquid	425 g
1 (14 ounce) can chicken broth	396 g
2 (15 ounce) cans Mexican stewed tomatoes	2 (425 g)
1 (8 ounce) can whole kernel corn	227 g
1 large onion, chopped	
1 sweet red bell pepper, chopped	
2 teaspoons minced garlic	10 ml
2 teaspoons ground cumin	10 ml
½ cup elbow macaroni	120 ml

- In skillet with a little oil, cook and brown turkey before placing in large slow cooker.

- Add beans, broth, tomatoes, corn, onion, bell pepper, garlic, cumin and a little salt and stir well.

- Cover and cook on LOW for 4 to 5 hours.

- Stir in macaroni and continue cooking for about 15 minutes. Stir to make sure macaroni does not stick to cooker and cook additional 15 minutes or until macaroni is tender. Serves 6 to 8.

TIP: Top each serving with dab of sour cream or 1 tablespoon (15 ml) shredded cheddar cheese.

Traditional Chili

2 pounds lean beef chili meat	1 kg
1 large onion, finely chopped	
1 (10 ounce) can chopped tomatoes and green chilies	280 g
2½ cups tomato juice	600 ml
2 tablespoons chili powder	30 ml
1 tablespoon ground cumin	15 ml
1 tablespoon minced garlic	15 ml
1 (15 ounce) can pinto or kidney beans	425 g

- In large slow cooker, combine chili meat, onion, tomatoes and green chilies, tomato juice, chili powder, cumin, garlic and 1 cup (240 ml) water and mix well.

- Cover and cook on LOW for 7 to 9 hours.

- Add pinto or kidney beans and continue to cook additional 30 minutes. Serves 4 to 6.

Easy Chili

4 pounds lean ground beef	**1.8 kg**
2 (10 ounce) packages hot chili mix	**2 (280 g)**
1 (6 ounce) can tomato sauce	**168 g**
2 (15 ounce) cans stewed tomatoes with liquid	**425 g**
2½ teaspoons ground cumin	**12 ml**

- In large skillet break ground beef into pieces and brown and drain. Use slotted spoon to drain fat and place beef in 5 to 6-quart (5 L) slow cooker.

- Add chili mix, tomato sauce, stewed tomatoes, cumin, 1 teaspoon (5 ml) salt and 1 cup (240 ml) water.

- Cover and cook on LOW setting for 4 to 5 hours. If you think you can't eat chili without beans, add 2 (15 ounce/425 g) cans ranch-style beans. Serves 6 to 8.

Chunky Chili

2 pounds premium cut stew meat	1 kg
1 onion, chopped	
2 (15 ounce) cans diced tomatoes	2 (425 g)
2 (15 ounce) cans pinto beans with liquid	2 (420 g)
1½ tablespoons chili powder	22 ml
2 teaspoons ground cumin	10 ml
1 teaspoon ground oregano	5 ml

- If stew meat is in fairly large chunks, cut each chunk in half.

- In large skillet, brown stew meat and transfer to large slow cooker.

- Add onion, tomatoes, beans, seasonings and a little salt.

- Cover and cook on LOW for 6 to 7 hours.

- Sprinkle shredded cheddar cheese over each serving. Serves 4 to 6.

Spit-Pea and Ham Chowder

1 medium potato	
3 cups cooked, cubed ham	710 ml
1 (16 ounce) bag split peas, rinsed	.5 kg
1 (11 ounce) can whole kernel corn with red and green peppers	312 g
1 (14 ounce) can chicken broth	396 g
2 carrots, sliced	
2 ribs celery, diagonally sliced	
1 tablespoon dried onion flakes	15 ml
1 teaspoon dried marjoram leaves	5 ml
1 teaspoon seasoned salt	5 ml

- Cut potato into small cubes and add to sprayed slow cooker.

- In slow cooker combine all ingredients plus 3 cups (710 ml) water and 1 teaspoon (5 ml) salt.

- Cover and cook on LOW for 6 to 8 hours. Serves 4 to 6.

Oyster Chowder

1 small sweet red bell pepper, chopped	
1 onion, chopped	
1 (14 ounce) can chicken broth	425 g
1 medium potato, cubed	
1 fresh jalapeno pepper, seeded, finely chopped	
8 ounces shucked oysters with liquid	227 g
1 (10 ounce) package frozen whole kernel corn, thawed	280 g
1 teaspoon dried oregano	5 ml
½ cup whipping cream	120 ml

- Combine all ingredients except cream in slow cooker.

- Cover and cook on LOW for 3 to 4 hours.

- When ready to serve, stir in cream. Serves 4.

Ham-Vegetable Chowder
A great recipe for leftover ham.

1 medium potato	
1 cup diced ham	
2 (10 ounce) cans cream of celery soup	2 (280 g)
1 (14 ounce) can chicken broth	396 g
3 cups finely diced ham	710 ml
1 (15 ounce) can whole kernel corn	425 g
2 carrots, sliced	
1 onion, coarsely chopped	
1 teaspoon dried basil	5 ml
1 teaspoon seasoned salt	5 ml
1 (10 ounce) package frozen broccoli florets	280 g

- Cut potato into 1-inch (2.5 cm) pieces.

- Combine 1 teaspoon (5 ml) pepper and all ingredients except broccoli florets in large slow cooker.

- Cover and cook on LOW for 5 to 6 hours. Add broccoli to cooker and cook for additional 1 hour. Serves 4 to 6.

TIP: If you don't like black specks in your chowder, use white pepper instead of black pepper.

Crab Chowder

2 small zucchini, thinly sliced	
1 sweet red bell pepper, julienned	
2 ribs celery, diagonally sliced	
1 medium potato, cubed	
2 tablespoons butter, melted	30 ml
1 (10 ounce) can chicken broth	280 g
1 teaspoon seasoned salt	5 ml
2 tablespoons cornstarch	30 ml
3 cups milk	710 ml
2 (6 ounce) cans crabmeat, drained	2 (168 g)
1 (3 ounce) package cream cheese, cubed	84 g

- Place zucchini, bell pepper, celery, potato, butter, broth and seasoned salt in sprayed slow cooker.

- Stir cornstarch into milk, stir and pour into slow cooker.

- Cover and cook on LOW for 3 to 4 hours.

- Turn heat to HIGH, add crabmeat and cream cheese and stir until cream cheese melts. Serves 4.

Country Chicken Chowder

1½ pounds boneless, skinless chicken breast halves	.7 kg
2 tablespoons butter	30 ml
2 (10 ounce) cans cream of potato soup	2 (280 g)
1 (14 ounce) can chicken broth	396 g
1 (8 ounce) package frozen whole kernel corn	227 g
1 onion, sliced	
2 ribs celery, sliced	
1 (10 ounce) package frozen peas and carrots, thawed	280 g
½ teaspoon dried thyme leaves	2 ml
½ cup half-and-half cream	120 ml

- Cut chicken into 1-inch (2.5 cm) strips.

- In skillet, brown chicken strips in butter and transfer to large slow cooker.

- Add soup, broth, corn, onion, celery, peas, carrots and thyme and stir.

- Cover and cook on LOW for 3 to 4 hours or until vegetables are tender.

- Turn off heat, stir in half-and-half cream and set aside for about 10 minutes before serving. Serves 4 to 6.

Corn-Ham Chowder

1 (14 ounce) can chicken broth	396 g
1 cup milk	240 ml
1 (10 ounce) can cream of celery soup	280 g
1 (15 ounce) can cream-style corn	425 g
1 (15 ounce) can whole kernel corn	425 g
½ cup dry potato flakes	120 ml
1 onion, chopped	
2 - 3 cups cooked, chopped ham	480 ml
	-710 ml

- In 6-quart (6 L) slow cooker, combine broth, milk, soup, cream-style corn, whole kernel corn, potato flakes, onion and ham.

- Cover and cook on LOW for 4 to 5 hours.

- When ready to serve, season with a little salt and pepper. Serves 4 to 6.

Chicken Chowder

3 cups cooked, cubed chicken	710 ml
1 (14 ounce) can chicken broth	396 g
2 (10 ounce) cans cream of potato soup	2 (280 g)
1 large onion, chopped	
3 ribs celery, sliced diagonally	
1 (16 ounce) package frozen whole kernel corn, thawed	.5 kg
⅔ cup whipping cream	160 ml

- In 5 to 6-quart (5 L) slow cooker combine chicken, chicken broth, potato soup, onion, celery, corn and ¾ cup (180 ml) water.

- Cover and cook on LOW for 3 to 4 hours.

- Add whipping cream to slow cooker and heat additional
  15 minutes or until thoroughly hot. Serves 4 to 6.

Shrimp and Ham Jambalaya

3 ribs celery, diagonally slice
1 onion, chopped
1 red and 1 green bell pepper, chopped
2 (15 ounce) cans stewed tomatoes   2 (425 g)
2 cups cooked, cubed smoked ham   480 ml
½ teaspoon cayenne pepper   2 ml
1 tablespoon dried parsley flakes   15 ml
2 teaspoons minced garlic   30 ml
1 pound peeled, veined shrimp   .5 kg

- Spray slow cooker, combine celery, onion, bell peppers, tomatoes, ham, cayenne pepper, parsley flakes, garlic and a little salt and pepper.

- Cover and cook on LOW for 7 to 8 hours or on HIGH for 3 to 4 hours.

- Stir in shrimp and cook on LOW 1 hour.

- Serve over hot, cooked rice. Serves 4 to 6.

Shrimp and Sausage Jambalaya

1 pound cooked, smoked sausage links	.5 kg
1 onion, chopped	
1 green bell pepper, chopped	
2 teaspoons minced garlic	
1 (28 ounce) can diced tomatoes	794 g)
1 tablespoon parsley flakes	15 ml
½ teaspoon dried thyme leaves	2 ml
1 teaspoon Cajun seasoning	5 ml
¼ teaspoon cayenne pepper	1 ml
1 pound peeled, veined shrimp	.5 kg
Hot cooked rice	

- Spray slow cooker, combine all ingredients except shrimp and rice.

- Cover and cook on LOW for 6 to 8 hours or on HIGH for 3 to 4 hours.

- Stir in shrimp and cook on LOW for additional 1 hour. Serve over hot, cooked rice. Serves 4 to 6.

Slow Cooker

Shrimp and Chicken Jambalaya

4 chicken breast halves, cubed	
1 (28 ounce) can diced tomatoes	794 g
1 onion, chopped	
1 green bell pepper, chopped	
1 (14 ounce) can chicken broth	396 g
½ cup dry white wine	120 ml
2 teaspoons dried oregano	10 ml
2 teaspoons Cajun seasoning	10 ml
½ teaspoon cayenne pepper	2 ml
1 pound cooked, peeled, veined shrimp	.5 kg
2 cups cooked white rice	480 ml

- Place all ingredients except shrimp and rice in slow cooker and stir.

- Cover and cook on LOW for 6 to 8 hours.

- Turn heat to HIGH, stir in shrimp and rice and cook additional 15 to 20 minutes. Serves 4 to 6.

VEGETABLES

Broccoli-Cheese Bake

4 tablespoons (½ stick) butter, melted	**60 ml**
1 (10 ounce) can cream of mushroom soup	**280 g**
1 (10 ounce) can cream of onion soup	**280 g**
1 cup instant rice	**240 ml**
1 (8 ounce) package cubed Velveeta® cheese	**227 g**
2 (10 ounce) packages frozen chopped broccoli, thawed	**2 (280 g)**

- Combine all ingredients, plus ½ cup (120 ml) water in sprayed slow cooker and stir well.

- Cover and cook on HIGH for 2 to 3 hours. Serves 4 to 6.

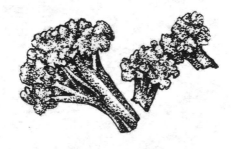

Broccoli and Cheese

2 (16 ounce) packages frozen broccoli florets, thawed	2 (425 g)
2 (15 ounce) cans whole new potatoes, drained	2 (425 g)
2 (10 ounce) cans cream of celery soup	2 (280 g)
½ cup milk	120 ml
1 (8 ounce) package shredded cheddar cheese, divided	227 g
1½ cups cracker crumbs	360 ml

- Place broccoli on plate, cut off stems and discard. In slow cooker, combine broccoli and potatoes.

- In saucepan, combine soup and milk, heat just enough to mix well and pour over broccoli and potatoes.

- Sprinkle half cheese and crumbs over broccoli.

- Cover and cook on LOW for 3 to 4 hours.

- When ready to serve, sprinkle remaining cheese and crumbs over top. Serves 6 to 8.

Savory Broccoli and Cauliflower

1 (16 ounce) package frozen broccoli florets, thawed	.5 kg
1 (16 ounce) package frozen cauliflower florets, thawed	.5 kg
2 (10 ounce) cans nacho cheese soup	2 (280 g)
6 slices bacon, cooked, crumbled	

- Place broccoli and cauliflower in sprayed slow cooker. Sprinkle with a little salt and pepper.

- Spoon soup over top and sprinkle with bacon. Cover and cook on LOW for 3 to 4 hours. Serves 6 to 8.

Company Broccoli

1½ pounds fresh broccoli, trimmed well	.7 kg
1 (10 ounce) can cream of chicken soup	280 g
½ cup mayonnaise	120 ml
1 (8 ounce) package shredded cheddar cheese	227 g
¼ cup toasted slivered almonds	60 ml

- Place broccoli in sprayed slow cooker.

- Combine chicken soup, mayonnaise, half the cheese and ¼ cup (60 ml) water. Spoon over broccoli.

- Cover and cook on LOW 2 to 3 hours. When ready to serve, sprinkle remaining cheese over broccoli and top with toasted almonds. Serves 6 to 8.

Sunshine Green Beans

2 (16 ounce) packages frozen whole green beans, thawed	2 (.5 kg)
2 (10 ounce) cans fiesta nacho cheese soup	2 (280 g)
1 (8 ounce) package seasoning blend onions and bell peppers	227 g
1 (8 ounce) can sliced water chestnuts, cut in half	227 g
1 teaspoon seasoned salt	5 ml

- Combine all ingredients plus ¼ cup (60 ml) water in large slow cooker and stir to mix well. Cover and cook on LOW for 4 to 5 hours. Serves 6 to 8.

Southern Green Beans and Potatoes

6 - 8 medium new potatoes with peels, sliced	
5 cups fresh whole green beans, trimmed	1.3 L
2 tablespoons dry, minced onions	30 ml
¼ cup (½ stick) butter, melted	60 ml
1 (10 ounce) can cream of celery soup	280 g
1 (10 ounce) can fiesta nacho cheese soup	280 g

- Place potatoes, green beans and minced onions in sprayed slow cooker. Pour melted butter over vegetables.

- In saucepan, combine both soups and ⅓ cup (80 ml) water. Heat just enough to be able to mix soups and pour over vegetables.

- Cover and cook on LOW for 7 to 8 hours. Serves 6 to 8.

Green Beans to Enjoy

2 pounds fresh green beans	1 kg
1 onion, finely chopped	
4 thick slices bacon	
5 - 6 medium new potatoes	
1 teaspoon sugar	5 ml

- Snap and wash green beans, place beans and onion in sprayed 5 to 6-quart (5 L) slow cooker.

- Cut bacon in 1-inch (2.5 cm) pieces and fry in skillet until crisp.

- Remove some of deeper "eyes" in new potatoes and cut into quarters.

- Add cooked bacon pieces and potatoes to cooker and 1 cup (240 ml) water.

- Add about 1½ teaspoons (7 ml) salt and sugar. (A touch of sugar always helps fresh vegetables.)

- Cover and cook on LOW for 3 to 4 hours. Serves 6 to 8.

Green Bean Revenge

2 (16 ounce) packages frozen whole green beans, thawed	2 (425 g)
2 (8 ounce) cans sliced water chestnuts, drained	2 (227 g)
1 (16 ounce) package cubed jalapeno Velveeta® cheese	425 g
1 (10 ounce) can tomatoes and green chilies	280 g
4 tablespoons (½ stick) butter, melted	60 ml
1 tablespoon chicken seasoning	15 ml
1½ cups slightly crushed potato chips	360 ml

- In slow cooker, combine green beans, water chestnuts, cheese, tomatoes and green chilies, melted butter and seasoning and mix well.

- Cover and cook on LOW for 3 to 5 hours. Just before serving, cover top with crushed potato chips. Serves 6 to 8.

TIP: If you would like this to be a one-dish meal, add 2 to 3 cups (480 ml) cooked, cubed ham.

Crunchy Green Beans

2 (16 ounce) packages frozen whole green beans, thawed	2 (.5 kg)
3 ribs celery, diagonally sliced	
1 sweet red bell pepper, julienned	
2 (11 ounce) cans sliced water chestnuts, drained	2 (312 g)
1 (10 ounce) can cream of chicken soup	280 g
½ cup slivered almonds	120 ml
1 (3 ounce) can french-fried onion rings	84 g

- In sprayed slow cooker, combine green beans, celery, bell pepper, water chestnuts, chicken soup and almonds.

- Cover and cook on LOW for 2 to 4 hours. About 10 minutes before serving, top with fried onion rings. Serves 6 to 8.

A Different Bean

3 (15 ounce) cans black beans, rinsed, drained	3 (425 g)
3 (15 ounce) cans great northern beans, rinsed, drained	3 (425 g)
1 (16 ounce) jar hot, thick-and-chunky salsa	.5 kg
½ cup packed brown sugar	120 ml

- Combine black beans, northern beans, salsa and brown sugar in 5 to 6-quart (5 L) slow cooker.

- Cover and cook on LOW for 3 to 4 hours.

- To include pinto beans in this dish, use only 2 cans black beans and 1 can pinto beans. Serves 6 to 8.

Beans and More Beans

4 thick slices bacon, cooked crisp, crumbled	
1 (15 ounce) can kidney beans, drained	425 g
1 (15 ounce) can lima beans with liquid	425 g
1 (15 ounce) can pinto beans with liquid	425 g
1 (15 ounce) can navy beans with liquid	425 g
1 (15 ounce) can pork and beans with liquid	425 g
1 onion, chopped	
¾ cup chili sauce	180 ml
1 cup packed brown sugar	240 ml
1 tablespoon Worcestershire sauce	15 ml

- In sprayed slow cooker, combine all ingredients and mix well.

- Cover and cook on LOW for 5 to 6 hours. Serves 6 to 8.

Better Butter Beans

2 cups sliced celery	480 ml
2 onions, chopped	
1 green bell pepper, julienned	
1 (15 ounce) can stewed tomatoes	425 g
¼ cup (½ stick) butter, melted	60 ml
1 tablespoon chicken seasoning	15 ml
3 (15 ounce) cans butter beans, drained	3 (425 g)

- In slow cooker, combine all ingredients and mix well.

- Cover and cook on LOW for 3 to 4 hours. Serves 6 to 8.

TIP: You can make this a one-dish dinner, add 2 to 3 cups (480 ml) cooked, cubed ham.

Italian Beans

2 (15 ounce) cans garbanzo beans, drained	2 (425 g)
1 (15 ounce) can red kidney beans, drained	425 g
1 (15 ounce) can cannellini beans, drained	425 g
2 (15 ounce) cans great northern beans, drained	2 (425 g)
1 teaspoon Italian seasoning	5 ml
1 (1 ounce) packet dry onion soup mix	28 g
1 teaspoon minced garlic	5 ml
½ cup beef broth	120 ml

- Combine all ingredients in slow cooker and stir well.
  Cover and cook on LOW for 5 to 6 hours or on
  HIGH for 2 hours 30 minutes to 3 hours.
  Serves 6 to 8.

Creamy Limas

2 (16 ounce) packages frozen baby lima beans, thawed	2 (.5 kg)
1 (10 ounce) can cream of celery	280 g
1 (10 ounce) can cream of onion soup	280 g
1 sweet red bell pepper, cored, seeded, julienned	
1 (4 ounce) jar sliced mushrooms, drained	114 g
¼ cup milk	60 ml
1 cup shredded cheddar-colby cheese	240 ml

- Combine lima beans, both soups, bell pepper,
  mushrooms and ½ teaspoon (2 ml) salt in saucepan
  and heat just enough to mix well. Pour into sprayed
  4 or 6-quart (4 L) slow cooker. Stir well.

- Cover and cook on LOW for 8 to 9 hours.

- Just before serving, stir in milk, remove limas to
  serving bowl and sprinkle cheese over top.
  Serves 6 to 8.

Chili Frijoles

2 cups dry pinto beans	480 ml
2 onions, finely chopped	
2 tablespoons chili powder	30 ml
1 teaspoon minced garlic	5 ml
1 (15 ounce) can tomato sauce	425 g
1½ pounds lean ground beef	.7 kg

- Soak beans overnight in water. Drain and transfer beans to large slow cooker. Add onion, chili powder, garlic, tomato sauce, 1 tablespoon (15 ml) salt and 8 cups (2 L) water.

- In skillet, brown ground beef, drain and transfer to cooker.

- Cover, cook on LOW for 8 to 9 hours or until beans are tender and stir occasionally. Serves 6 to 8.

TIP: If you forget to soak beans overnight, here's Plan B. Place beans in large saucepan and cover with water. Bring to a boil, turn off heat and let stand 1 hour.

Cajun Beans and Rice

1 pound dry black or kidney beans	.5 kg
2 onions, chopped	
2 teaspoons minced garlic	10 ml
1 tablespoon ground cumin	15 ml
1 (14 ounce) can chicken broth	396 g)
1 cup instant brown rice	240 ml

- Place beans in saucepan, cover with water and soak overnight.

- In 4 or 5-quart (4 L) slow cooker, combine beans, onion, garlic, cumin, chicken broth, 2 teaspoons (10 ml) salt and 2 cups (480 ml) water.

- Cover and cook on LOW for 4 to 6 hours.

- Stir in instant rice, cover and cook additional 20 minutes. Serves 4 to 6.

TIP: If soaking beans overnight is not an option, place beans in saucepan and add enough water to cover by 2 inches (5 cm). Bring to a boil, reduce heat and simmer for 10 minutes. Let stand 1 hour, drain and rinse beans.

Cinnamon Carrots

2 (16 ounce) packages baby carrots	**2 (.5 kg)**
¾ cup packed brown sugar	**180 ml**
¼ cup honey	**60 ml**
½ cup orange juice	**120 ml**
2 tablespoons butter, melted	**30 ml**
¾ teaspoon ground cinnamon	**4 ml**

- Place carrots in sprayed 3 to 4-quart (3 L) slow cooker.

- In bowl, combine brown sugar, honey, orange juice, butter and cinnamon and mix well. Pour over carrots and mix so sugar-cinnamon mixture coats carrots.

- Cover and cook on LOW for 3 hours 30 minutes to 4 hours and stir twice during cooking time.

- About 20 minutes before serving, transfer carrots with slotted spoon to serving dish and cover to keep warm.

- Pour liquid from cooker into saucepan; boil for several minutes until liquid reduces by half. Spoon over carrots in serving dish. Serves 6 to 8.

Krazy Karrots

1 (16 ounce) package baby carrots	.5 kg
¼ cup (½ stick) butter, melted	60 ml
⅔ cup packed brown sugar	160 ml
1 (1 ounce) packet ranch dressing mix	28g

- In 4-quart (4 L) slow cooker, combine carrots, melted butter, brown sugar, ranch dressing mix and ¼ cup (60 ml) water and stir well.

- Cover and cook on low for 3 to 4 hours and stir occasionally. Serves 4.

Squash Combo

1½ pounds small yellow squash	.7 kg
1½ pounds zucchini	.7 kg
1 teaspoon seasoned salt	5 ml
¼ cup (½ stick) butter, melted	60 ml
½ cup seasoned dried breadcrumbs	120 ml
½ cup shredded cheddar cheese	120 ml

- Cut both yellow squash and zucchini in small pieces.

- Place in sprayed slow cooker and sprinkle with seasoned salt and pepper.

- Pour melted butter over squash and sprinkle with breadcrumbs and cheese.

- Cover and cook on LOW for 5 to 6 hours. Serves 6 to 8.

Sunny Yellow Squash

2 pounds medium yellow squash, sliced	1 kg
2 onions, coarsely chopped	
3 ribs celery, diagonally sliced	
1 green bell pepper, cored, seeded, julienned	
1 (8 ounce) package cream cheese, cubed	227 g
1 teaspoon sugar	5 ml
¼ cup (½ stick) butter, melted	60 ml
1 (10 ounce) can cheddar cheese soup	280 g
1½ cups seasoned breadcrumbs	360 ml

- In slow cooker, combine all ingredients, except croutons and mix well. Add 1 teaspoon (5 ml) each of salt and pepper.

- Cover and cook on LOW for 3 to 4 hours. Before serving, sprinkle top with croutons. Serves 6 to 8.

Tip: If you don't like black specks, use white pepper instead of black pepper.

Golden Squash

1 pound yellow squash, thinly sliced	.5 kg
1 pound zucchini, thinly sliced	.5 kg
3 ribs celery, sliced	
1 onion, chopped	
1 (10 ounce) can cream of chicken soup	280 g
1 (8 ounce) carton sour cream	227 g
3 tablespoons flour	45 ml
1 (6 ounce) package seasoned stuffing mix	168 g
½ cup (1 stick) butter, melted	120 ml

- In large bowl, combine squash, zucchini, celery, onion and soup.

- Mix sour cream with flour and stir into vegetables. Toss stuffing with melted butter and spoon half into slow cooker.

- Top with vegetables and spoon remaining stuffing on top.

- Cover and cook on LOW for 5 to 7 hours. Serves 6 to 8.

Super Corn

2 (15 ounce) cans whole kernel corn	2 (425 g)
2 (15 ounce) cans creamed corn	2 (425 g)
½ cup (1 stick) butter, melted	120 ml
1 (8 ounce) carton sour cream	227 g
1 (8 ounce) package jalapeno cornbread mix	227 g

- In large bowl, combine all ingredients and mix well.

- Pour into sprayed slow cooker, cover and cook on LOW for 4 to 5 hours. Serves 6 to 8.

TIP: Make this a one-dish meal by adding 2 to 3 cups (480 ml) leftover, cubed ham.

Yummy Corn

1 (8 ounce) and 1 (3 ounce) package cream cheese	227 g/84 g
½ cup (1 stick) butter, melted	120 ml
2 (16 ounce) packages frozen whole kernel corn, thawed	2 (.5 kg)

- In sprayed 4-quart (4 L) slow cooker, turn cooker to HIGH and add cream cheese and butter.

- Cook just until cheese and butter melt and stir. Add corn and a little salt and pepper.

- Cover and cook on LOW for 1 hour 30 minutes to 2 hours. Serves 4 to 6.

Creamed Peas and Potatoes

2 pounds small new potatoes with peels, quartered 1 kg
2 (10 ounce) cans fiesta nacho cheese soup   2 (280 g)
½ cup milk   120 ml
1 (16 ounce) package frozen green peas with pearl
**   onions, thawed   .5 kg**

- Sprinkle potatoes with a little salt and pepper, place in sprayed slow cooker and place peas on top.

- In saucepan, combine nacho cheese soup and milk, heat just enough to mix well and spoon over peas.

- Cover and cook on LOW for 4 to 5 hours.
  Serves 6 to 8.

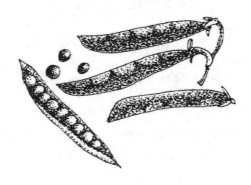

Creamed-Cheese Spinach

2 (10 ounce) packages frozen chopped spinach	280 g
1 (16 ounce) carton small curd cottage cheese	.5 kg
1½ cups shredded American or cheddar cheese	360 ml
3 eggs, beaten	
¼ cup (½ stick) butter, melted	60 ml
¼ cup flour	60 ml

- Drain spinach with paper towels and press out all liquid with paper towels.

- In mixing bowl, combine all ingredients and mix well. Spoon into sprayed slow cooker.

- Cover and cook on HIGH for 1 hour, change heat to LOW and cook additional 3 to 5 hours or until knife inserted in center comes out clean. Serves 4 to 6.

Cheese-Please Spinach

1 (10 ounce) and 1 (16 ounce) package chopped	
spinach, thawed, drained	280 g/.5 kg
1 (8 ounce) package cream cheese, cubed, softened	227 g
1 (10 ounce) can cream of chicken soup	280 g
1 egg, beaten	
1 (8 ounce) package shredded cheddar cheese	227 g

- Drain spinach with paper towels and press out all liquid.

- In large bowl, combine spinach, cream cheese, chicken soup, egg and a little salt and pepper. Spoon into sprayed slow cooker.

- Cover and cook on LOW for 3 to 4 hours.

- Before serving, stir in cheddar cheese. Serves 4 to 6.

Healthy Veggies

1 (16 ounce) package frozen broccoli, cauliflower	
and carrots	.5 kg
2 medium zucchini, halved lengthwise, sliced	
1 (1 ounce) packet ranch dressing mix	28 g
2 tablespoons butter, melted	30 ml

- Place broccoli, cauliflower, carrots and zucchini in 4-quart (4 L) slow cooker.

- Combine ranch dressing mix, melted butter and ½ cup (120 ml) water, spoon over vegetables and stir.

- Cover and cook on LOW for 2 to 3 hours. Serves 4.

Harvest-Vegetable Casserole

3 - 4 medium new potatoes with peels, sliced	
2 onions, sliced	
3 carrots, sliced	
2 cups chopped green cabbage	480 ml
¼ cup Italian dressing	60 ml
1 (1 pound) kielbasa sausage	.5 kg
1 (15 ounce) can Italian stewed tomatoes	425 g

- In large, sprayed slow cooker, place potatoes, onions, carrots and cabbage.

- Cut sausage into 1-inch (2.5 cm) pieces and place on top of vegetables.

- Drizzle stewed tomatoes in even layers over vegetables.

- Cover and cook on LOW for 6 to 8 hours or until vegetables are tender. Serves 4 to 6.

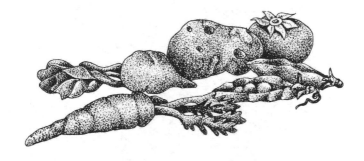

California Vegetables

1 (16 ounce) package frozen vegetable mix, thawed	.5 kg
1 (10 ounce) package frozen green peas, thawed	280 g
1 (10 ounce) package frozen whole kernel corn, thawed	280 g
2 (10 ounce) cans cream of mushroom soup	2 (280 g)
1 cup instant white rice	240 ml
1 (8 ounce) carton cubed Velveeta® cheese	227 g
1 cup milk	240 ml
2 tablespoons butter, melted	30 ml
1 teaspoon seasoned salt	5 ml

- Place all vegetables in large, sprayed slow cooker.

- In saucepan, combine soup, rice, cheese, milk, butter, seasoned salt and 1 cup (240 ml) water, heat just enough to mix and pour over vegetables.

- Cover and cook on LOW for 4 to 5 hours. Stir before serving. Serves 6 to 8.

Golden Veggies

1 (16 ounce) package frozen cauliflower florets, thawed	.5 kg
1 (15 ounce) can whole kernel corn	425 g
¾ pound small yellow squash, chopped	340 g
¼ cup (½ stick) butter, melted	60 ml
2 (10 ounce) cans cheddar cheese soup	2 (280 g)
6 slices bacon, cooked, crumbled	

- Place cauliflower, corn and squash in sprayed slow cooker and sprinkle with a little salt and pepper.

- Pour melted butter over vegetables and spoon cheese soup on top. Sprinkle with crumbled bacon.

- Cover and cook on LOW for 4 to 5 hours. Serves 4 to 6.

Four Veggie Bake

1 (10 ounce) package frozen broccoli florets, thawed	280 g
1 (10 ounce) package frozen cauliflower, thawed	280 g
1 (10 ounce) package frozen brussels sprouts	280 g
4 small yellow squash, sliced	
1 (10 ounce) can cream of mushroom soup	280 g
1 (16 ounce) package cubed Velveeta® cheese	.5 kg

- Place vegetables in sprayed slow cooker.

- Layer soup and cheese on top of vegetables.

- Cover and cook on LOW for 3 to 4 hours. Serves 4 to 6.

Potatoes al Grande

6 medium potatoes, peeled	
1 (8 ounce) package shredded cheddar cheese,	
** divided**	**227 g**
1 (10 ounce) can cream of chicken soup	**280 g**
¼ cup (½ stick) butter, melted	**60 ml**
1 (8 ounce) carton sour cream	**227 g**
1 (3 ounce) can french-fried onion rings	**84 g**

- Cut potatoes in 1-inch (2.5 cm) strips. Toss potatoes with a little salt and pepper plus 2 cups (480 ml) cheese. Place in slow cooker.

- Combine soup, melted butter and 2 tablespoons (30 ml) water in saucepan and heat just enough to pour over potato mixture.

- Cover and cook on LOW for 6 to 8 hours or until potatoes are tender.

- Stir in sour cream and remaining cheese.

- When ready to serve, sprinkle onion rings over top of potatoes. Serves 4 to 6.

Pretty Parsley Potatoes

2 pounds new potatoes with peels, quartered	**1 kg**
¼ cup vegetable oil	**60 ml**
1 (1 ounce) packet ranch dressing mix	**28 g**
¼ cup chopped fresh parsley	**60 ml**

- Place potatoes, vegetable oil, dressing mix and ¼ cup (60 ml) water in 4 to 5-quart (4 L) slow cooker and toss to coat potatoes.

- Cover and cook on LOW for 3 to 4 hours or until potatoes are tender.

- When ready to serve, sprinkle parsley over potatoes and toss. Serves 4 to 6.

Roasted New Potatoes

18 - 20 new potatoes with peels	
¼ cup (½ stick) butter, melted	**60 ml**
1 tablespoon dried parsley	**15 ml**
½ teaspoon garlic powder	**2 ml**
½ teaspoon paprika	**2 ml**

- Combine all ingredients plus ½ teaspoon (2 ml) each of salt and pepper in sprayed slow cooker and mix well.

- Cover and cook on LOW for 7 hours or on HIGH for 3 hours 30 minutes to 4 hours.

- When ready to serve, remove potatoes with slotted spoon to serving dish and cover to keep warm.

- Add about 2 tablespoons (30 ml) water to drippings and stir until they blend well.

- Pour mixture over potatoes. Serves 4 to 6.

Good Old Cheesy Potatoes

1 (28 ounce) package frozen hashbrown potatoes with onions and peppers, thawed	794 g
2 (10 ounce) cans cream of chicken soup	2 (280 g)
1 (8 ounce) carton sour cream	227 g
½ cup (1 stick) butter, melted, divided	120 ml
1 (8 ounce) package shredded cheddar cheese	227 g
2 tablespoons dried parsley	30 ml
2 cups dry stuffing mix	480 ml

- In large bowl, combine potatoes, soup, sour cream, ¼ cup (60 ml) melted butter, cheese, parsley and 1 teaspoon (5 ml) salt and mix well.

- Spoon mixture into large slow cooker. Sprinkle stuffing mix over potato mixture and drizzle remaining butter over stuffing.

- Cover and cook on LOW for 7 to 9 hours or on HIGH for 3 to 4 hours. Serves 4 to 6.

Glory Potatoes

1 (10 ounce) can cream of chicken soup	280 g
1 (8 ounce) carton sour cream	227 g
2 pounds potatoes, peeled, cubed	1 kg
1 (8 ounce) package shredded cheddar Jack cheese	227 g
1 cup crushed potato chips	240 ml

- In bowl combine soup, sour cream, some salt and pepper and ¼ cup (60 ml) water.

- Combine potatoes and cheese in 5-quart (5 L) slow cooker. Spoon soup-sour cream mixture over potatoes.

- Cover and cook on LOW for 8 to 9 hours.

- When ready to serve, sprinkle crushed potato chips over potatoes. Serves 4 to 6.

Easy Baked Potatoes

10 medium russet potatoes with peels
¼ - ½ cup oil   **60 ml**
Butter
Sour cream

- Pierce potatoes with fork. Brush potato skins with oil and sprinkle a little salt and pepper on potato skins.

- Wrap potatoes individually in foil and place in large slow cooker.

- Cover and cook on LOW for 7 to 8 hours or until potatoes are tender.

- Prepare assorted toppings such as: shredded cheese, salsa, ranch dip, chopped green onions, bacon bits, chopped boiled eggs, cheese-hamburger dip, broccoli-cheese soup, etc. Serves 4.

Dressed-Up Hashbrowns

1 (26 ounce) package frozen hashbrown potatoes with onions and peppers	737 g
2 - 3 cups cooked, chopped ham	480 ml
1 (16 ounce) carton sour cream	.5 kg
1 (8 ounce) package shredded cheddar Jack cheese	227 g
1 (3 ounce) can french-fried onion rings	84 g

- In large skillet, cook potatoes in a little oil. Transfer to 5 to 6-quart (5 L) slow cooker.

- Combine ham, sour cream and cheese and mix into hash browns.

- Cover and cook on LOW for 2 to 3 hours.

- Dress potatoes up by sprinkling onion rings on top of cheese. Serves 4 to 6.

Creamed New Potatoes

2 - 2½ pounds new potatoes with peels, quartered	1 kg
1 (8 ounce) package cream cheese, softened	227 g
1 (10 ounce) can fiesta nacho soup	280 g
1 (1 ounce) packet buttermilk ranch salad dressing mix	28 g
1 cup milk	240 mL

- Place potatoes in 6-quart (6 L) slow cooker.

- With mixer, beat cream cheese until creamy and fold in fiesta nacho soup, ranch salad dressing mix and milk. Stir into potatoes.

- Cover and cook on LOW for 3 to 4 hours or until potatoes are well done. Serves 4 to 6.

Company Potatoes

1 (5 ounce) box scalloped potatoes	143 g
1 (5 ounce) box au gratin potatoes	143 g
1 cup milk	240 ml
6 tablespoons (¾ stick) butter, melted	90 ml
½ pound bacon, cooked crisp, crumbled	227 g

- Place both boxes of potatoes in sprayed slow cooker. In bowl combine milk, butter and 4¼ cups (1.2 L) water and pour over potatoes.

- Cover and cook on LOW for 4 to 5 hours.

- When ready to serve, sprinkle crumbled bacon over top of potatoes. Serves 4 to 6.

Cheezy Potatoes

1 (28 ounce) bag frozen diced potatoes with onions and peppers, thawed	794 g
1 (8 ounce) package shredded Monterey Jack and cheddar cheese blend	227 g
1 (10 ounce) can cream of celery soup	280 g
1 (8 ounce) carton sour cream	227 g

- In sprayed 5 or 6-quart (5 L) slow cooker, combine potatoes, cheese, soup, sour cream and 1 teaspoon (5 ml) pepper and mix well.

- Cover and cook on LOW 4 to 6 hours. Stir well before serving. Serves 6 to 8.

Cheesy Ranch Potatoes

2½ pounds new potatoes with peels, quartered	1.2 kg
1 onion, cut into 8 parts	
1 (10 ounce) can fiesta nacho cheese soup	280 g
1 (8 ounce) carton sour cream	227 g
1 (1 ounce) packet dry ranch salad dressing mix	28 g
Chopped fresh parsley, optional	

- Place potatoes and onion in sprayed 4 to 5-quart (4 L) slow cooker.

- In bowl, combine, nacho cheese, sour cream and dressing mix and whisk well to mix.

- Cover and cook on LOW for 6 to 7 hours.

- To serve, sprinkle chopped fresh parsley over potato mixture. Serves 4 to 6.

Sweet Potatoes and Pineapple

3 (15 ounce) cans sweet potatoes, drained	**3 (425 g)**
½ (20 ounce) can pineapple pie filling	**½ (567 g)**
2 tablespoons butter, melted	**30 ml**
½ cup packed brown sugar	**120 ml**
½ teaspoon cinnamon	**2 ml**

- Place sweet potatoes, pie filling, melted butter, brown sugar and cinnamon in sprayed 4 to 5-quart (4 L) slow cooker and lightly stir.

- Cover and cook on LOW for 2 to 3 hours. Serves 6 to 8.

Topping:

1 cup packed light brown sugar	**240 ml**
3 tablespoons butter, melted	**45 ml**
½ cup flour	**120 ml**
1 cup coarsely chopped nuts	**240 ml**

- While potatoes cook, combine topping ingredients, spread out on foil-lined baking pan and bake at 350° (176° C) for 15 to 20 minutes.

- When ready to serve, sprinkle topping over sweet potatoes.

Glazed Sweet Potatoes

3 (15 ounce) cans sweet potatoes, drained	
¼ cup (½ stick) butter, melted	60 ml
2 cups packed brown sugar	480 ml
⅓ cup orange juice	80 ml
½ teaspoon ground cinnamon	2 ml

- After draining sweet potatoes, cut into smaller chunks and place them in 4 to 5-quart (4 L) slow cooker.

- Add butter, brown sugar, orange juice, a little salt and a sprinkle of cinnamon and stir well.

- Cover and cook on LOW for 4 to 5 hours.
  Serves 4 to 6.

Hoppin' John

3 (15 ounce) cans black-eyed peas with liquid	3 (425 g)
1 onion, chopped	
1 (6.2 ounce) package parmesan-butter rice	168 g
2 cups cooked, chopped ham	480 ml
2 tablespoons butter, melted	30 ml

- In slow cooker, combine peas, onion, rice mix, ham, butter and 1¾ cups (420 ml) water and mix well.

- Cover and cook on LOW for 2 to 4 hours.
  Serves 6 to 8.

Spicy Spanish Rice

1½ cups white rice	360 ml
1 (10 ounce) can diced tomatoes and green chilies	280 g
1 (15 ounce) can stewed tomatoes	425 g
1 (1 ounce) packet taco seasoning	28 g
1 large onion, chopped	

- In 5-quart (5 L) slow cooker, combine all ingredients plus 2 cups (480 ml) water and stir well.

- Cover and cook on LOW for 5 to 7 hours. (The flavor will go through the rice better if you stir 2 or 3 times during cooking time.) Serves 4.

TIP: Make this "a main dish" by slicing 1 pound (.5 kg) Polish sausage slices to rice mixture.

Delicious Risotto Rice

1½ cups Italian risotto rice	360 ml
3 (14 ounce) cans chicken broth	3 (396 g)
3 tablespoons butter, melted	45 ml
1½ cups sliced, fresh mushrooms	360 ml
1 cup sliced celery	240 ml

- In 4 to 5-quart (4 L) slow cooker, combine rice, broth, butter, mushrooms and celery.

- Cover and cook on LOW for 2 to 3 hours or until rice is tender. Serves 4 to 6.

Crunchy Couscous
When rice is boring, try couscous.

1 (10 ounce) box original plain couscous	280 g
2 cups sliced celery	480 ml
1 sweet red bell pepper, chopped	
1 yellow bell pepper, chopped	
1 (16 ounce) jar creamy alfredo sauce	.5 kg

- In 5-quart (5 L) slow cooker, combine couscous, celery, chopped bell peppers, alfredo sauce and 1½ cups (360 ml) water and mix well.

- Cover and cook on LOW for 2 hours, stir once or twice. Check slow cooker to make sure celery and peppers are cooked, but still crunchy. Serves 4 to 6.

Carnival Couscous

1 (5.7 ounce) box herbed-chicken couscous	155 g
1 red bell pepper, julienned	
1 green bell pepper, julienned	
2 small yellow squash, sliced	
1 (16 ounce) package frozen mixed vegetables, thawed	.5 kg
1 (10 ounce) can French onion soup	280 g
¼ cup (½ stick) butter, melted	60 ml
½ teaspoon seasoned salt	2 ml

- In sprayed slow cooker, combine all ingredients with 1½ cups (360 ml) water and mix well.

- Cover and cook on LOW for 2 to 4 hours. Serves 4.

Cheese-Spaghetti and Spinach

1 (7 ounce) box ready-cut spaghetti	198 g
2 tablespoons butter	30 ml
1 (8 ounce) carton sour cream	227 g
1 cup shredded cheddar cheese	240 ml
1 (8 ounce) package Monterey Jack cheese, divided	227 g
1 (12 ounce) package frozen, chopped spinach, thawed, very well drained	340 g
1 (6 ounce) can cheddar french-fried onions	168 g

- Cook spaghetti according to package directions, drain and stir in butter until it melts.

- In large bowl, combine sour cream, cheddar cheese, half Monterey Jack cheese, spinach and half can onions.

- Fold into spaghetti and spoon into sprayed slow cooker.

- Cover and cook on LOW for 2 to 4 hours.

- When ready to serve, sprinkle remaining Jack cheese and fried onion rings over top. Serves 4.

St. Pat's Noodles

1 (12 ounce) package medium noodles	340 g
1 cup half-and-half cream	240 ml
1 (10 ounce) package frozen chopped spinach, thawed	280 g
6 tablespoons (¾ stick) butter, melted	90 ml
2 teaspoons seasoned salt	10 ml
1½ cups shredded cheddar-Monterey Jack cheese	360 ml

- In saucepan, cook noodles according to package directions and drain.

- Place in 5 to 6-quart (5 L) slow cooker. Add half-and-half cream, spinach, butter and seasoned salt and stir until they blend well.

- Cover and cook on LOW for 2 to 3 hours.

- When ready to serve, fold in cheese. Serves 4.

CHICKEN

Chicken Olé

6 boneless, skinless chicken breast halves
1 (8 ounce) package cream cheese, softened   **227g**
1 (16 ounce) jar salsa   **.5 kg**
2 teaspoons cumin   **10 ml**
1 bunch fresh green onions with tops, chopped

- Pound chicken breasts to flatten. In mixing bowl, beat cream cheese until smooth, add salsa, cumin and onions and mix gently.

- Place heaping spoonfuls of cream cheese mixture on each chicken breast and roll. (There will be leftover cream cheese mixture.)

- Place chicken breast seam side-down in sprayed slow cooker. Spoon remaining cream cheese mixture over each chicken roll.

- Cover and cook on LOW for 5 to 6 hours. Serves 4 to 6.

Chicken for the Gods

1¾ cups flour	420 ml
Scant 2 tablespoons dry mustard	30 ml
6 boneless, skinless chicken breast halves	
2 tablespoons oil	30 ml
1 (10 ounce) can chicken-rice soup	280 g

- Place flour and mustard in shallow bowl and dredge chicken to coat all sides.

- In skillet, brown chicken breasts in oil. Place all breasts in 6-quart (6 L) oval slow cooker.

- Pour chicken and rice soup over chicken and add about ¼ cup (60 ml) water.

- Cover and cook on LOW for 6 to 7 hours.
  Serves 4 to 6.

Apricot Chicken

6 boneless, skinless chicken breasts halves	
1 (12 ounce) jar apricot preserves	340g
1 (8 ounce) bottle Catalina dressing	227 g
1 (1 ounce) packet dry onion soup mix	28 g

- Place chicken in sprayed 6-quart (6 L) slow cooker.

- Combine apricot preserves, Catalina dressing, onion soup mix and ¼ cup (60 ml) water and stir well. Cover chicken breasts with sauce mixture.

- Cover and cook on LOW for 5 to 6 hours.
  Serves 4 to 6.

Artichoke-Chicken Pasta

1½ pounds boneless, skinless chicken breast tenders	.7 kg
1 (15 ounce) can artichoke hearts, quartered	425 g
¾ cup chopped, roasted, red peppers	180 ml
1 (8 ounce) package American cheese, shredded	227 g
1 tablespoon white wine Worcestershire sauce	15 ml
1 (10 ounce) can cream of chicken soup	280 g
1 (8 ounce) package shredded cheddar cheese	227 g
4 cups hot, cooked bow-tie pasta	1 L

- In slow cooker, combine chicken tenders, artichoke, roasted peppers, American cheese, Worcestershire sauce and soup and mix well.

- Cover and cook on LOW for 6 to 8 hours. About 20 minutes before serving, fold in cheddar cheese, hot pasta and a little salt and pepper. Serves 4.

Broccoli-Rice Chicken

1¼ cups converted rice	300 ml
2 pounds boneless, skinless chicken breast halves	1 kg
Dried parsley	
1 (1.8 ounce) packet cream of broccoli soup mix	70 g
1 (14 ounce) can chicken broth	396 g

- Place rice in lightly sprayed slow cooker. Cut chicken into slices and put over rice. Sprinkle with parsley and a little pepper.

- In saucepan, combine soup mix and chicken broth and 1 cup (240 ml) water. Heat just enough to mix well. Pour over chicken and rice. Cover and cook on LOW for 6 to 8 hours. Serves 4 to 6.

Bacon-Wrapped Chicken

1 (2.5 ounce) jar dried beef	**70 g**
6 boneless, skinless chicken breast halves	
6 slices bacon	
2 (10 ounce) cans golden mushroom soup	**2 (280 g)**
1 (6 ounce) package parmesan-butter rice, cooked	**168 g**

- Place dried beef sliced in 5-quart (5 L) slow cooker.

- Roll each chicken breast half in slice of bacon and place over dried beef.

- In saucepan heat soup and ⅓ cup (80 ml) water just enough to mix well and pour over chicken.

- Cover and cook on LOW for 7 to 8 hours.

- Serve over hot, cooked rice. Serves 4 to 6.

Broccoli-Cheese Chicken

4 boneless, skinless chicken breast halves	
2 tablespoons butter, melted	30 ml
1 (10 ounce) can broccoli-cheese soup	280 g
¼ cup milk	60 ml
1 (10 ounce) package frozen broccoli spears	280 g

- Dry chicken breasts with paper towels and place in sprayed, oval slow cooker.

- In bowl, combine melted butter, soup and milk and spoon over chicken. Cover and cook on LOW for 4 to 6 hours.

- Remove cooker lid and place broccoli over chicken. Cover and cook an additional 1 hour. Serve over hot, buttered rice. Serves 4.

Cream Cheese Chicken

4 boneless, skinless chicken breast halves	
2 tablespoons butter, melted	30 ml
1 (10 ounce) can cream of mushroom soup	280 g
2 tablespoons dried Italian salad dressing	30 ml
½ cup sherry	120 ml
1 (8 ounce) package cream cheese, cubed	227 g

- Wash chicken breasts, dry with paper towels and brush melted butter over chicken. Place in sprayed, oval slow cooker and add remaining ingredients.

- Cover and cook on LOW for 6 to 7 hours. Serve over hot, buttered noodles. Serves 4.

Chicken and Noodles

2 pounds boneless, skinless chicken breast halves	**1 kg**
¼ cup cornstarch	**60 ml**
⅓ cup soy sauce	**80 ml**
2 onions, chopped	
3 ribs celery, sliced diagonally	
1 sweet red bell pepper, julienned	
2 (14 ounce) cans mixed Chinese vegetables,	
drained	**2 (396 g)**
¼ cup molasses	**60 ml**

- Place chicken breasts and 2 cups (480 ml) water in sprayed slow cooker. Cover and cook on LOW for 3 to 4 hours. At least 1 hour before serving, remove chicken and cut into bite-size pieces.

- In bowl, combine cornstarch and soy sauce and mix well. Stir into slow cooker. Add onions, celery, bell pepper, mixed vegetables and molasses.

- Turn heat to HIGH and cook for 1 to 2 hours.

- Serve over chow mein noodles. Serves 4 to 6.

Chicken and Pasta

1 (16 ounce) package frozen whole green beans, thawed	.5 kg
1 onion, chopped	
1 cup fresh mushroom halves	240 ml
3 boneless, skinless chicken breast halves	
1 (15 ounce) can Italian stewed tomatoes	425 g
1 teaspoon chicken bouillon granules	5 ml
1 teaspoon minced garlic	5 ml
1 teaspoon Italian seasoning	5 ml
1 (8 ounce) package fettuccine	227 g
1 (4 ounce) package grated parmesan cheese	114 g

- Place green beans, onion and mushrooms in sprayed 4-quart (4 L) slow cooker.

- Cut chicken into 1-inch (2.5 cm) pieces and place over vegetables.

- In small bowl, combine stewed tomatoes, chicken bouillon, garlic and Italian seasoning. Pour over chicken.

- Cover and cook on LOW for 5 to 6 hours.

- Cook fettuccine according to package directions and drain.

- Serve chicken over fettuccine sprinkled with parmesan cheese. Serves 4.

TIP: Add ¼ cup (60 ml) butter to make this dish have a richer taste.

Chicken and Vegetables

4 - 5 boneless, skinless chicken breast halves	
2 teaspoons seasoned salt	10 ml
1 (16 ounce) package frozen broccoli, cauliflower and carrots, thawed	.5 kg
1 (10 ounce) can cream of celery soup	280 g
1 (8 ounce) package shredded cheddar- Jack cheese	227 g

- Cut chicken into strips, sprinkle with seasoned salt and place in sprayed slow cooker.

- In large bowl, combine vegetables, celery soup and half cheese and mix well. Spoon over chicken breasts.

- Cover and cook on LOW for 4 to 5 hours.

- About 10 minutes before serving, sprinkle remaining cheese on top of casserole. Serves 4 to 6.

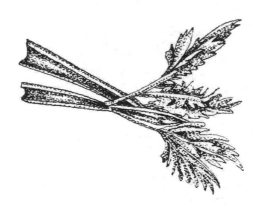

Chicken Curry over Rice

3 large boneless, skinless chicken breast halves	
½ cup chicken broth	**120 ml**
1 (10 ounce) can cream of chicken soup	**227 g**
1 onion, coarsely chopped	
1 sweet red bell pepper, julienne	
¼ cup golden raisins	**60 ml**
1½ teaspoons curry powder	**7 ml**
¼ teaspoon ground ginger	**1 ml**

- Cut chicken into thin strips and place in sprayed 5 to 6-quart (5 L) slow cooker. Combine broth, soup, onion, bell pepper, raisins, curry powder and ginger and mix well. Pour over chicken.

- Cover and cook on LOW for 3 to 4 hours. Serve over hot, cooked rice. Serves 4.

Chicken Delicious

5 - 6 boneless skinless chicken breast halves
1 (16 ounce) package frozen broccoli florets,
thawed .5 kg
1 sweet red bell pepper, julienned
1 (16 ounce) jar parmesan-mozzarella cheese
creation sauce .5 kg
3 tablespoons sherry 45 ml

- In skillet, brown chicken breasts and place in sprayed, 5 to 6-quart (5 L) oval slow cooker.

- Place broccoli florets on plate, remove much of stem and discard.

- In bowl combine broccoli florets, bell pepper, cheese sauce and sherry and mix well. Spoon over chicken breasts.

- Cover and cook on LOW for 4 to 5 hours. Serve over hot, buttered noodles. Serves 4 to 6.

Chicken Delight

¾ cup white rice	180 ml
1 (14 ounce) can chicken broth	396 g
1 (1 ounce) package dry onion soup mix	28 g
1 sweet red bell pepper, seeded, chopped	
2 (10 ounce) cans cream of celery soup	2 (280 g)
¾ cup white cooking wine	180 ml
4 - 6 boneless skinless chicken breast halves	
1 (3 ounce) package fresh parmesan cheese	84 g

- In bowl, combine rice, broth, soup mix, bell pepper, celery soup, ¾ cup (180 ml) water, wine and several sprinkles of black pepper and mix well. (Make sure to mix soup well with liquids.)

- Spray, 6-quart (6 L) oval slow cooker and place chicken breasts in cooker.

- Pour rice-soup mixture over chicken breasts.

- Cover and cook on LOW for 4 to 6 hours.

- One hour before serving, sprinkle parmesan cheese over chicken. Serves 4 to 6.

Chicken Dinner

1 cup rice	**240 ml**
1 tablespoon chicken seasoning	**15 ml**
1 (1 ounce) packet dry onion soup mix	**28 g**
1 green bell pepper, seeded, chopped	
1 (4 ounce) jar diced pimentos, drained	**113 g**
¾ teaspoon dried basil	**4 ml**
1 (14 ounce) can chicken broth	**396 g**
1 (10 ounce) can cream of chicken soup	**280 g**
5 - 6 boneless, skinless chicken breast halves	

- In bowl, combine rice, chicken seasoning, onion soup mix, bell pepper, pimentos, basil, broth, ½ cup (120 ml) water and chicken soup and mix well.

- Place chicken breasts in sprayed, oval slow cooker and cover with rice mixture.

- Cover and cook on LOW for 6 to 7 hours. Serves 4 to 6.

Chicken Fajitas

2 pounds boneless, skinless chicken breast halves	**1 kg**
1 onion, thinly sliced	
1 sweet red bell pepper, cored, seeded, julienned	
1 teaspoon ground cumin	**5 ml**
1½ teaspoons chili powder	**7 ml**
1 tablespoon lime juice	**15 ml**
½ cup chicken broth	**120 ml**
8 - 10 warm flour tortillas	
Guacamole	
Sour cream	
Lettuce and tomatoes	

- Cut chicken into diagonal strips and place in sprayed slow cooker. Top with onion and bell pepper.

- In bowl, combine cumin, chili powder, lime juice and chicken broth and pour over chicken and vegetables.

- Cover and cook on LOW for 5 to 7 hours.

- Serve several slices of chicken mixture with sauce into center of each warm tortilla and fold.

- Serve with guacamole, sour cream, lettuce or tomatoes or plain. Serves 4 to 6.

Chicken for Supper

5 - 6 boneless, skinless chicken breast halves	
6 carrots, cut in 1-inch length	2.5 cm
1 (15 ounce) can cut green beans, drained	425 g
1 (15 ounce) can whole new potatoes, drained	425 g
2 (10 ounce) cans cream of mushroom soup	2 (280 g)
Shredded cheddar cheese	

- Wash, dry chicken breasts with paper towels and place in sprayed, oval slow cooker.

- In bowl, combine, carrots, green beans, potatoes and mushroom soup and pour over chicken in cooker.

- Cover and cook on LOW for 8 to 10 hours. When ready to serve, sprinkle cheese over top. Serves 4 to 6.

Chicken-Ready Supper

1 (6 ounce) package stuffing mix	168 g
3 cups cooked, chopped chicken breasts	710 ml
1 (16 ounce) package frozen whole green beans,	
thawed	.5 kg
2 (12 ounce) jars chicken gravy	2 (340 g)

- Prepare stuffing mix according to package directions and place in oval slow cooker.

- Follow with layer of chopped chicken or leftover turkey breasts and place green beans over chicken. Pour chicken gravy over green beans.

- Cover and cook on LOW for 3 hours 30 minutes to 4 hours. Serves 4 to 6.

Chicken Marseilles

4 - 5 boneless, skinless chicken breast halves	
2 tablespoons butter	30 ml
1 (1.8 ounce) packet leek soup and dip mix	57 g
½ teaspoon dill weed	2 ml
1 cup milk	240 ml
¾ cup sour cream	180 ml
Cooked brown rice	

- Place chicken breasts in large, sprayed slow cooker.

- In saucepan, combine butter, leek soup mix, dill weed, milk and ½ cup (120 ml) water and heat just enough for butter to melt and ingredients to mix well. Pour over chicken.

- Cover and cook on LOW for 3 to 5 hours.

- When ready to serve, remove chicken breasts to platter with hot, cooked brown rice and cover to keep warm.

- Add sour cream to cooker liquid and stir well. Pour sauce over chicken and rice. Serves 4 to 5.

Chicken Breast Deluxe

4 slices bacon	
5 - 6 boneless, skinless chicken breast halves	
1 cup sliced celery	240 ml
1 cup sliced red bell pepper	240 ml
1 (10 ounce) can cream of chicken soup	280 g
2 tablespoons white wine or cooking wine	30 ml
6 slices Swiss cheese	
2 tablespoons dried parsley	30 ml

- In large skillet, cook bacon, drain, crumble and reserve drippings. Place chicken in skillet with bacon drippings and lightly brown on both sides. Transfer chicken to sprayed, oval slow cooker and place celery and red bell pepper over chicken.

- In same skillet, combine soup and wine, stir and spoon over vegetables and chicken. Cover and cook on LOW for 3 to 4 hours. Top with slices of cheese over each chicken breast and cook for additional 10 minutes.

- Serve with creamy sauce and sprinkle with crumbled bacon. Serves 4 to 6.

Chicken Supper

5 boneless, skinless chicken breast halves
1 (16 ounce) jar alfredo sauce .5 kg
1 (16 ounce) package frozen green peas, thawed .5 kg
1½ cups shredded mozzarella cheese 360 ml
Hot buttered noodles

- Cut chicken into strips and place in sprayed slow cooker.

- In bowl, combine alfredo sauce, peas and cheese and mix well. Spoon over chicken strips.

- Cover and cook on LOW for 5 to 6 hours.

- When ready to serve, spoon over hot, cooked noodles. Serves 4 to 5.

TIP: If you want chicken supper in 1 casserole, cook 1 (8 ounce/227 g) package noodles and mix with chicken and peas. Sprinkle a little extra cheese over top and serve.

Chicken-Supper Ready

6 medium new potatoes with peels, quartered	
4 - 5 carrots	
4 - 5 boneless, skinless chicken breast halves	
1 tablespoon chicken seasoning	15 ml
2 (10 ounce) cans cream of chicken soup	2 (280 g)
⅓ cup white wine or cooking wine	80 ml

- Cut carrots into ½-inch (1.2 cm) pieces. Place potatoes and carrots in slow cooker.

- Sprinkle chicken breasts with chicken seasoning and place over vegetables.

- In saucepan heat soups and ¼ cup (60 ml) water just to mix and pour over chicken and vegetables.

- Cover and cook on LOW for 5 to 6 hours. Serves 4 to 5.

TIP: Use 1 (10 ounce/280 g) can chicken soup and 1 (10 ounce/280 g) can mushroom soup for a tasty change.

Chow Mein Chicken

4 boneless, skinless chicken breast halves	
2 - 3 cups sliced celery	
1 onion, coarsely chopped	
⅓ cup soy sauce	**80 ml**
¼ teaspoon cayenne pepper	
1 (14 ounce) can chicken broth	**396 g**
1 (16 ounce) can bean sprouts, drained	**.5 kg**
1 (8 ounce) can water chestnuts, drained	**227 g**
1 (6 ounce) can bamboo shoots	**168 g**
¼ cup flour	**60 ml**

- Combine chicken, celery, onion, soy sauce, cayenne pepper and chicken broth in sprayed slow cooker. Cover and cook on LOW for 3 to 4 hours.

- Add bean sprouts, water chestnuts and bamboo shoots to chicken. Mix flour and ¼ cup (60 ml) water and stir into chicken and vegetables. Cook for additional 1 hour. Serve over chow mein noodles. Serves 4.

Classy Chicken Dinner

1 (6 ounce) box long grain-wild rice	168 g
12 - 15 frozen chicken breast tenderloins, thawed	
1 (16 ounce) jar roasted garlic-parmesan cheese creation	.5 kg
1 cup frozen petite green peas, thawed	240 ml

- Pour 2½ cups (600 ml) water, rice and seasoning packet in sprayed 5-quart (5 L) slow cooker and stir well.

- Spoon in cheese creation and mix well. Place chicken tenderloins in slow cooker and cover with green peas.

- Cover and cook on LOW for 4 to 5 hours. Serves 4.

Creamy Chicken and Potatoes

4 boneless, skinless chicken breast halves	
2 teaspoons chicken seasoning	10 ml
8 - 10 small new potatoes with peels	
1 (10 ounce) can cream of chicken soup	280 g
1 (8 ounce) carton sour cream	227 g

- Place chicken breast halves, sprinkled with chicken seasoning in slow cooker. Arrange new potatoes around chicken.

- Combine soup, sour cream and good amount of black pepper. Spoon over chicken breasts.

- Cover and cook on LOW for 4 to 6 hours. Serves 4.

Creamed Chicken

4 large boneless, skinless chicken breast halves
Lemon juice
1 sweet red bell pepper, chopped
2 ribs celery, sliced diagonally
1 (10 ounce) can cream of chicken soup   **280 g**
1 (10 ounce) can cream of celery soup   **280 g**
⅓ cup dry white wine   **80 ml**
1 (4 ounce) package shredded parmesan cheese   **114 g**

- Wash and pat chicken dry with paper towels, rub a little lemon juice over chicken and sprinkle with a little salt and pepper.

- Place in sprayed slow cooker and top with celery.

- In saucepan, combine soups and wine and heat just enough to mix thoroughly.

- Pour over chicken breasts and sprinkle with parmesan cheese.

- Cover and cook on LOW for 6 to 7 hours.

- Serve over hot, buttered rice. Serves 4 to 5.

Creamed Chicken and Vegetables

4 large boneless, skinless chicken breast halves
1 (10 ounce) can cream of chicken soup   **280 g**
1 (16 ounce) package frozen peas and carrots,
    thawed   **.5 kg**
1 (12 ounce) jar chicken gravy   **340 g**

- Cut chicken in thin slices. Spray 6-quart (6 L) slow cooker.

- Pour soup and ½ cup (120 ml) water into slow cooker, mix and add chicken slices.

- Sprinkle a little salt and lots of pepper over chicken and soup.

- Cover and cook on LOW for 4 to 5 hours.

- Add peas, carrots, chicken gravy and another ½ cup (120 ml) water. Increase heat to HIGH and cook for about 1 hour or until peas and carrots are tender.

- Serve over large, refrigerated buttermilk biscuits or over Texas toast (thick slices of bread). Serves 4.

Creamy Salsa Chicken

4 - 5 boneless, skinless chicken breast halves	
1 (1 ounce) packet dry taco seasoning mix	**28 g**
1 cup salsa	**240 ml**
½ cup sour cream	**120 ml**

- Place chicken breasts in sprayed 5 to 6-quart (5 L) slow cooker and add ¼ cup (60 ml) water.

- Sprinkle taco seasoning mix over chicken and top with salsa. Cook on LOW for 5 to 6 hours.

- When ready to serve, remove chicken breasts and place on platter. Stir sour cream into salsa sauce and spoon over chicken breasts. Serves 4 to 5.

Delightful Chicken and Veggies

4 - 5 boneless, skinless chicken breast halves	
1 (15 ounce) can whole kernel corn, drained	**425 g**
1 (10 ounce) box frozen green peas, thawed	**280 g**
1 (16 ounce) jar alfredo sauce	**.5 kg**
1 teaspoon chicken seasoning	**5 ml**
1 teaspoon minced garlic	**5 ml**

- Brown chicken breasts in skillet and place in sprayed, oval slow cooker. Combine corn, peas, alfredo sauce, ¼ cup (60 ml) water, chicken seasoning and minced garlic and spoon mixture over chicken breasts.

- Cover and cook on LOW for 4 to 5 hours. Serve over hot, cooked pasta. Serves 4 to 5.

Slow Cooker Cordon Bleu

4 boneless, skinless chicken breast halves
4 slices cooked ham
4 slices Swiss cheese, softened
1 (10 ounce) can cream of chicken soup   280 g
¼ cup milk   60 ml

- Place chicken breasts on cutting board and pound until breast halves are thin.

- Place ham and cheese slices on chicken breasts, roll and secure with toothpick.

- Arrange chicken rolls in sprayed 4-quart (4 L) slow cooker.

- Pour chicken soup with milk into saucepan, heat just enough to mix well and pour over chicken rolls.

- Cover and cook on LOW for 4 to 5 hours.

- Serve over hot, cooked noodles and cover with sauce from soup. Serves 4.

Delicious Chicken Pasta

1 pound chicken tenders	**.5 kg**
Lemon-herb chicken seasoning	
3 tablespoons butter	**45 ml**
1 onion, coarsely chopped	
1 (15 ounce) can diced tomatoes	**425 g**
1 (10 ounce) can golden mushroom soup	**280 g**
1 (8 ounce) box angel hair pasta	**227 g**

- Pat chicken tenders dry with several paper towels and sprinkle ample amount of chicken seasoning. Melt butter in large skillet, brown chicken and place in oval slow cooker. Pour remaining butter and seasonings over chicken and cover with onion.

- In separate bowl, combine diced tomatoes and mushroom soup and pour over chicken and onions. Cover and cook on LOW for 4 to 5 hours. When ready to serve, cook pasta according to package directions. Serve chicken and sauce over pasta. Serves 4.

Farmhouse Supper

1 (8 ounce) package medium noodles	227 g
4 - 5 boneless, skinless chicken breast halves	
1 (14 ounce) can chicken broth	396 g
2 cups sliced celery	480 ml
2 onions, chopped	
1 green bell pepper, seeded, chopped	
1 red bell pepper, seeded, chopped	
1 (10 ounce) can cream of chicken soup	280 g
1 (10 ounce) can cream of mushroom soup	280 g
1 cup shredded 4-cheese blend	240 ml

- Cook noodles in boiling water until barely tender and drain well.

- Cut chicken into thin slices and brown lightly in skillet with a little oil

- Mix noodles, chicken and broth in large, sprayed slow cooker.

- Make sure noodles separate and coat with broth. Stir in remaining ingredients.

- Cover and cook on LOW for 4 to 6 hours. Serves 4 to 5.

Golden Chicken Dinner

6 medium new potatoes with peels, cubed	
6 medium carrots, chopped	
5 boneless, skinless chicken breast halves	
1 tablespoon dried parsley flakes	15 ml
1 teaspoon seasoned salt	5 ml
1 (10 ounce) can golden mushroom soup	280 g
1 (10 ounce) can cream of chicken soup	280 g
4 tablespoons dried mashed potato flakes	60 ml
Water or milk	

- Cut chicken into ½-inch (1.2 cm) pieces.

- Place potatoes and carrots in slow cooker and top with chicken breasts.

- Sprinkle parsley flakes, seasoned salt and ½ teaspoon (2 ml) pepper over chicken. Combine soups and spread over chicken.

- Cover and slow cook on LOW for 6 to 7 hours.

- Stir in potato flakes and a little water or milk if necessary to make gravy and cook additional 30 minutes. Serves 4 to 6.

Hawaiian Chicken

6 boneless, skinless chicken breast halves	
1 (15 ounce) can pineapple slices with juice	425 g
⅓ cup packed brown sugar	80 ml
2 tablespoons lemon juice	30 ml
¼ teaspoon ground ginger	1 ml
¼ cup cornstarch	60 ml

- Place chicken breasts in sprayed, oval slow cooker and sprinkle with a little salt. Place pineapple slices over chicken.

- In small bowl, combine pineapple juice, brown sugar, lemon juice, ginger and cornstarch and stir until cornstarch mixes with liquids. Pour over chicken breasts.

- Cover and cook on LOW for 4 to 5 hours or on HIGH for 2 hour 30 minutes to 3 hours. Serve over hot, buttered rice. Serves 4 to 6.

Imperial Chicken

1 (6 ounce) box long grain-wild rice	168 g
1 (16 ounce) jar roasted garlic-parmesan cheese creation	.5 kg
6 boneless, skinless chicken breast halves	
1 (16 ounce) box frozen French-style green beans, thawed	.5 kg
½ cup slivered almonds, toasted	120 ml

- Spray, oval slow cooker and pour in 2½ cups (600 ml) water, rice and seasoning packet and stir well. Spoon in cheese creation and mix well. Place chicken breasts in slow cooker and cover with green beans. Cover and cook on LOW for 3 to 5 hours. When ready to serve, sprinkle with slivered almonds. Serves 4 to 6.

Here's the Stuff

5 boneless, skinless chicken breast halves	
2 (10 ounce) cans cream of chicken soup	**280 g**
1 (6 ounce) box chicken stuffing mix	**168 g**
1 (16 ounce) package frozen green peas, thawed	**.5 kg**

- Place chicken breasts in 6-quart (6 L) slow cooker and spoon soups over chicken.

- Combine stuffing mix with ingredients on package directions, include seasoning packet and spoon over chicken and soup.

- Cover and cook on LOW for 5 to 6 hours.

- Sprinkle drained green peas over top of stuffing. Cover and cook additional 45 to 50 minutes. Serves 4 to 5.

TIP: Use 1 (10 ounce/280 g) can cream of chicken soup and 1 (10 ounce/280 g) can fiesta nacho soup for a nice variation.

Mushroom Chicken

4 boneless, skinless chicken breasts halves	
1 (15 ounce) can tomato sauce	425 g
2 (4 ounce) cans sliced mushrooms, drained	2 (114 g)
1 (10 ounce) package frozen seasoning blend	
onions and peppers	280 g
2 teaspoons Italian seasoning	10 ml
1 teaspoon minced garlic	5 ml

- In skillet brown chicken breasts and place in oval slow cooker.

- In bowl combine tomato sauce, mushrooms, onions, peppers, Italian seasoning, minced garlic and ¼ cup (60 ml) water and spoon over chicken breasts.

- Cover and cook on LOW for 4 to 5 hours. Serves 4.

Orange Chicken

6 boneless, skinless chicken breast halves	
1 (12 ounce) jar orange marmalade	340 g
1 (8 ounce) bottle Russian salad dressing	227 g
1 (1 ounce) packet dry onion soup mix	28 g

- Place chicken breasts in oval slow cooker. Combine orange marmalade, dressing, soup mix and ¾ cup (180 ml) water and stir well.

- Spoon mixture over chicken breasts. Cover and cook on LOW for 4 to 6 hours. Serves 4 to 6.

Oregano Chicken

½ cup (1 stick) butter, melted	120 ml
1 (1 ounce) packet dry Italian salad dressing	28 g
1 tablespoon lemon juice	15 ml
4 - 5 boneless, skinless chicken breast halves	
2 tablespoons dried oregano	30 ml

- In bowl, combine butter, dressing and lemon juice and mix well. Place chicken breasts in large, sprayed slow cooker. Spoon butter-lemon juice mixture over chicken.

- Cover and cook on LOW for 5 to 6 hours.

- One hour before serving, baste chicken with pan juices and sprinkle oregano over chicken. Serves 4 to 6.

Quick-Fix Chicken

4 - 6 boneless, skinless chicken breast halves	
1 (8 ounce) carton sour cream	225 g
¼ cup soy sauce	60 ml
2 (10 ounce) cans French onion soup	2 (280 g)

- Wash and dry chicken with paper towels and place in sprayed, oval slow cooker. Combine sour cream, soy sauce and onion soup, stir and mix well.

- Cover and cook on LOW for 5 to 6 hours if chicken breasts are large; 3 to 4 hours if breasts are medium. Serves 4 to 6.

Tip: Serve chicken and sauce with hot, buttered rice or mashed potatoes.

Perfect Chicken Breasts

1 (2.5 ounce) jar dried beef	70 g
6 small boneless, skinless chicken breast halves	
6 slices bacon	
2 (10 ounce) cans golden mushroom soup	2 (280 g)

- Line bottom of oval slow cooker with slices of dried beef and overlap some.

- Roll each chicken breast with slice of bacon and secure with toothpick. Place in slow cooker, overlapping as little as possible.

- Combine mushroom soup and ½ cup (120 ml) water or milk and spoon over chicken breasts.

- Cover and cook on LOW for 6 to 8 hours. Serves 4 to 6.

When cooked, you will have a great "gravy" that is wonderful served over noodles or rice.

Picante Chicken

4 boneless, skinless chicken breast halves	
1 green bell pepper, seeded, cut in rings	
1 (16 ounce) jar picante sauce	.5 kg
⅓ cup packed brown sugar	80 ml
1 tablespoon mustard	15 ml

- Place chicken breasts in slow cooker with bell pepper rings over top of chicken. Combine picante, brown sugar and mustard and spoon over top of chicken. Cover and cook on LOW for 4 to 5 hours. Serves 4.

Russian Chicken

1 (8 ounce) bottle Russian salad dressing	227 g
1 (16 ounce) can whole cranberry sauce	.5 kg
1 (1 ounce) packet dry onion soup mix	28 g
4 chicken quarters, skinned	

- In bowl, combine salad dressing, cranberry sauce, ½ cup (120 ml) water and soup mix. Stir well to get all lumps out of soup mix.

- Place 4 chicken pieces in sprayed, 6-quart (6 L) oval slow cooker and spoon dressing-cranberry mixture over chicken.

- Cover and cook on LOW for 4 to 5 hours. Serve sauce and chicken over hot, cooked rice. Serves 4 to 6.

TIP: Use 6 chicken breasts if you don't want to cut-up a chicken.

So-Good Chicken

4 - 5 boneless, skinless chicken breast halves	
1 (10 ounce) can golden mushroom soup	280 g
1 cup white cooking wine	240 ml
1 (8 ounce) carton sour cream	227 g

- Wash, dry chicken breasts with paper towels and sprinkle a little salt and pepper over each.

- In bowl, whisk together mushroom soup, wine and sour cream and mix well. Spoon over chicken breasts. Cover and cook on LOW for 5 to 7 hours. Serves 4 to 6.

Winter Dinner

1 pound chicken tenderloins	.5 kg
1 pound Polish sausage	.5 kg
2 onions, chopped	
1 (31 ounce) can pork and beans with liquid	1 kg
1 (15 ounce) can ranch-style beans, drained	425 g
1 (15 ounce) can great northern beans	425 g
1 (15 ounce) can butter beans, drained	425 g
1 cup ketchup	240 ml
1 cup packed brown sugar	240 ml
1 tablespoon vinegar	15 ml
6 slices bacon, cooked, crumbled	

- In skillet, brown chicken slices in a little oil and place in large, sprayed slow cooker. Add sausage, cut in 1-inch (2.5 cm) pieces, onions, 4 cans beans, ketchup, brown sugar and vinegar and stir gently.

- Cover and cook on LOW for 7 to 8 hours or on HIGH for 3 hours 30 minutes to 4 hours. When ready to serve, sprinkle crumbled bacon over top. Serves 4 to 6.

Savory Chicken Fettuccine

2 pounds boneless, skinless chicken thighs, cubed	1 kg
½ teaspoon garlic powder	2 ml
1 sweet red bell pepper, chopped	
2 ribs celery, chopped	
1 (10 ounce) can cream of celery soup	280 g
1 (10 ounce) can cream of chicken soup	280 g
1 (8 ounce) package cubed Velveeta° cheese	227 g
1 (4 ounce) jar diced pimentos	114 g
1 (16 ounce) package spinach fettuccine	.5 kg

- Place cubed chicken pieces in slow cooker. Sprinkle with garlic powder, ½ teaspoon (2 ml) pepper, bell pepper and celery. Top with condensed soups.

- Cover and cook on HIGH for 4 to 6 hours or until chicken juices are clear. Stir in cheese and pimentos. Cover and cook until cheese melts.

- Cook fettuccine according to package directions and drain. Place fettuccine in serving bowl and spoon chicken over fettuccine. Serve hot. Serves 4 to 6.

Scrumptious Chicken Breasts

There is a lot of delicious sauce.

5 - 6 boneless, skinless chicken breast halves	
1 teaspoon chicken seasoning	5 ml
1 (10 ounce) can cream of chicken soup	280 g
1 (10 ounce) can broccoli-cheese soup	280 g
½ cup white cooking wine	120 ml

- Place breast halves, sprinkled with black pepper and chicken seasoning, in sprayed oval slow cooker.

- In saucepan, combine soups and wine and heat enough to mix well. Pour over chicken.

- Cover and cook on LOW for 5 to 6 hours.

- Serve chicken and sauce over hot, cooked noodles. Serves 4 to 6.

TIP: This is great served with roasted garlic, oven-baked Italian toast.

TIP: If chicken breasts are very large, cut in half lengthwise.

Smothered Chicken Breasts

4 boneless, skinless chicken breast halves
1 (10 ounce) can French onion soup   **280 g**
2 teaspoons chicken seasoning   **10 ml**
1 (4 ounce) jar sliced mushrooms, drained   **114 g**
1 cup shredded mozzarella cheese   **240 ml**
Chopped green onions

- In skillet brown each chicken breast and place in sprayed, oval slow cooker.

- Pour onion soup over chicken and sprinkle black pepper and chicken seasoning over chicken breasts.

- Place mushrooms and cheese over chicken breasts.

- Cover and cook on LOW for 4 to 5 hours. To give this chicken a really nice touch when ready to serve, sprinkle some chopped green onions over each serving. Serves 4.

Southwestern Chicken Pot

6 boneless, skinless chicken breast halves	
1 teaspoon ground cumin	5 ml
1 teaspoon chili powder	5 ml
1 (10 ounce) can cream of chicken soup	280 g
1 (10 ounce) can fiesta nacho cheese soup	280 g
1 cup salsa	240 ml

- In sprayed, oval slow cooker, place chicken breasts sprinkled with cumin, chili powder and a little salt and pepper.

- In saucepan, combine soups and salsa. Heat just enough to mix and pour over chicken breasts. Cover and cook on LOW for 6 to 7 hours. Serve over hot, cooked rice with warmed, flour tortillas spread with butter. Serves 4 to 6.

Sweet-and-Sour Chicken

6 boneless, skinless chicken breast halves	
Oil	
1 (1 ounce) packet dry onion soup mix	28 g
1 (6 ounce) can frozen orange juice concentrate, thawed	168 g

- In skillet, brown chicken breasts in little oil and place in large, sprayed slow cooker.

- In bowl, combine onion soup mix, orange juice concentrate and ½ cup (120 ml) water and pour over chicken. Cover and cook on LOW for 3 to 5 hours. Serves 4 to 6.

Sunday Chicken

4 large boneless, skinless chicken breast halves
Chicken seasoning
4 slices American cheese
1 (10 ounce) can cream of celery soup   **280 g**
½ cup sour cream   **120 ml**
1 (6 ounce) box chicken stuffing mix   **168 g**
½ cup (1 stick) butter, melted   **120 ml**

- Wash and dry chicken breasts with paper towels and place in sprayed, oval slow cooker. Sprinkle each breast with chicken seasoning.

- Place slice of cheese over each chicken breast.

- Combine celery soup and sour cream, mix well and spoon over chicken and cheese.

- Sprinkle chicken stuffing mix over top of cheese. Drizzle melted butter over stuffing mix.

- Cover and cook on LOW for 5 to 6 hours. Serves 4.

Tasty Chicken-Rice and Veggies

4 boneless, skinless chicken breast halves
2 (10 ounce) jars sweet-and-sour sauce   **2(280 g)**
1 (16 ounce) package frozen broccoli, cauliflower and carrots,
    thawed   **.5 kg**
1 (10 ounce) package frozen baby peas, thawed   **280 g**
2 cups sliced celery 480ml
1 (6 ounce) package parmesan-butter mix   **168 g**
⅓ cup toasted, slivered almonds 80ml

- Cut cchicken in 1-inch (2.5cm) strips.

- Combine pieces, sweet-and-sour sauce and all vegetables in sprayed 6-quart (6L) slow cooker.

- Cover and cook on LOW for 4 to 6 hours.

- When ready to serve, cook parmesan-butter rice according to directions on package and fold in almonds

- Serve chicken and vegetables over hot, cooked rice. Serves 4.

Honey-Baked Chicken

2 small fryer chickens, quartered
½ cup (1 stick) butter, melted   **120 ml**
⅔ cup honey   **160 ml**
¼ cup dijon-style mustard   **60 ml**
1 teaspoon curry powder   **5 ml**

- Place chicken pieces in large slow cooker, skin-side up and sprinkle a little salt over chicken.

- In bowl, combine butter, honey, mustard and curry powder and mix well.

- Pour butter-mustard mixture over chicken quarters.

- Cover and cook on LOW for 6 to 8 hours. Baste chicken once during cooking. Serves 6 to 8.

Tangy Chicken

1 large fryer chicken, quartered
2 tablespoons butter   **30 ml**
½ cup Heinz 57® sauce   **120 ml**
1 (15 ounce) can stewed tomatoes   **425 g**

- Wash, dry chicken quarters with paper towels and place in large slow cooker.

- In saucepan, combine butter, 57 sauce and stewed tomatoes. Heat just until butter melts and ingredients mix well. Pour over chicken.

- Cover and cook on LOW for 5 to 6 hours. Serves 4 to 6.

Chicken with Orange Sauce

1 whole chicken, quartered	
½ cup plus 2 tablespoons flour	**120 ml/ 30 ml**
½ teaspoon ground nutmeg	**2 ml**
½ teaspoon cinnamon	**2 ml**
2 large sweet potatoes, peeled, sliced	
1 (8 ounce) can pineapple chunks with juice	**227 g**
1 (10 ounce) can cream of chicken soup	**280 g**
⅔ cup orange juice	**160 ml**

- Wash and dry chicken quarters with paper towels. In bowl combine ½ cup (120 ml) flour, nutmeg and cinnamon and coat chicken. Place sweet potatoes and pineapple in large, sprayed slow cooker. Arrange chicken on top.

- In bowl, combine chicken soup, orange juice and remaining flour and pour over chicken.

- Cover and cook on LOW for 7 to 9 hours or on HIGH for 3 to 4 hours.

- Serve over hot, buttered rice. Serves 4 to 6.

Tasty Chicken and Veggies

1 (2½ - 3 pound) whole chicken, quartered	1.2 kg
1 (16 ounce) package baby carrots	.5 kg
4 potatoes, peeled, sliced	
3 ribs celery, sliced	
1 onion, peeled, sliced	
1 cup Italian salad dressing	240 ml
⅔ cup chicken broth	160 ml

- Rinse, dry and place chicken quarters in sprayed 6-quart (6 L) slow cooker with carrots, potatoes, celery and onion.

- Pour salad dressing and chicken broth over chicken and vegetables. Cover and cook on LOW for 6 to 8 hours. Serves 4 to 6.

TIP: When serving, garnish with sprigs of fresh parsley.

"Baked" Chicken

1 cup white rice	240 mL
2 (10 ounce) cans cream of chicken soup	2 (280 g)
1 (14 ounce) can chicken broth	1 (396 g)
1(1.2 ounce) packet dry onion soup mix	1 (28 g)
1 chicken, quartered packet	

- Place rice in 5 to 6-quart (6 L) oval slow cooker.

- In saucepan, combine chicken soup, broth, 2 soup cans water (500 mL) and onion soup mix and mix well. Heat just enough to mix ingredients.

- Spoon half over rice and place 4 chicken quarters in slow cooker. Spoon remaining soup mixture over chicken. Cover and cook on LOW for 5 to 6 hours. Serves 4 to 6.

Saffron Rice and Chicken

1 fryer-broiler chicken, quartered	
½ teaspoon garlic powder	2 ml
1 (14 ounce) can chicken broth	396 g
1 onion, chopped	
1 green and 1 yellow bell pepper, cored, seeded, quartered	
1 (4 ounce) jar pimentos, drained	114 g
⅓ cup prepared bacon bits	80 ml
2 tablespoons butter, melted	30 ml
1 (5 ounce) package saffron yellow rice mix	143 g

- Sprinkle chicken with garlic powder and a little salt and pepper.

- In skillet, brown chicken quarters in little oil. Place chicken in sprayed, oval slow cooker and pour broth in slow cooker.

- Combine, onion, bell peppers, pimentos and bacon bits and spoon over chicken quarters.

- Cover and cook on LOW for 4 to 5 hours.

- Carefully remove chicken quarters from cooker, stir in rice mix and butter and return chicken to cooker.

- Cover and cook 1 hour or until rice is tender. Serves 4 to 6.

Lemon Chicken

1 (2½ - 3 pound) chicken, quartered	1.2 kg
1 teaspoon dried oregano	5 ml
2 teaspoons minced garlic	10 ml
2 tablespoons butter	30 ml
¼ cup lemon juice	60 ml

- Season chicken quarters with salt, pepper and oregano and rub garlic on chicken.

- In skillet, brown chicken quarters on all sides in butter and transfer to sprayed, oval slow cooker.

- Add ⅓ cup (80 ml) water to skillet, scrape bottom and pour over chicken.

- Cover and cook on LOW for 6 to 8 hours.

- At last hour of cooking, pour lemon juice over chicken, finish cooking. Serves 4 to 6.

Chicken Coq Vin

1 large fryer chicken, quartered, skinned	
Oil	
10 - 12 small white onions, peeled	
½ pound whole mushrooms	**227 g**
1 teaspoon minced garlic	**5 ml**
½ teaspoon dried thyme leaves	**2 ml**
10 - 12 small new potatoes with peels	
1 (10 ounce) can chicken broth	**280 g**
1 cup burgundy wine	**240 ml**
6 bacon slices, cooked, crumbled	

- In skillet, brown chicken quarters on both sides and set aside.

- Place white onions, whole mushrooms, garlic and thyme in sprayed, oval slow cooker.

- Add chicken quarters, potatoes, chicken broth and a little salt and pepper.

- Cover and cook on LOW for 8 to 10 hours or on HIGH for 3 to 4 hours.

- During last hour, turn heat to HIGH, add wine and continue cooking.

- Sprinkle crumbled bacon over chicken before serving. Serves 4 to 6.

Chicken Cacciatore

2 onions, thinly sliced	
1 (2½ - 3) pound fryer chicken, quartered	1.2 kg
2 (6 ounce) cans tomato paste	2 (168 g)
1 (4 ounce) can sliced mushrooms	114 g
1½ teaspoons minced garlic	7 ml
½ teaspoon dried basil	2 ml
2 teaspoons oregano leaves	10 ml
⅔ cup dry white wine	160 ml

- Place sliced onions in sprayed, oval slow cooker. Wash, dry chicken quarters with paper towels and place in slow cooker.

- In bowl, combine tomato paste, mushrooms, garlic, basil, oregano and wine and pour over chicken quarters. Cover and cook on LOW for 7 to 8 hours or on HIGH for 4 hours. Serves 4 to 6.

Taco Chicken

3 cups cooked, chopped chicken	710 ml
1 (1 ounce) packet taco seasoning	28 g
1 cup white rice	240 ml
2 cups chopped celery	480 ml
1 green bell pepper, seeded, chopped	
2 (15 ounce) cans Mexican stewed tomatoes	2 (425 g)

- Combine chicken, taco seasoning, rice, celery, bell pepper and stewed tomatoes and mix well. Pour into 5-quart (5 L) slow cooker. Cover and cook on LOW for 4 to 5 hours. Serves 4 to 6.

TIP: This is a great recipe for leftover chicken.

Monterey Bake

6 (6 inch) corn tortillas	6 (15 cm)
3 cups leftover cubed chicken	710 ml
1 (10 ounce) package frozen whole kernel corn	280 g
1 (15 ounce) can pinto beans with liquid	425 g
1 (16 ounce) hot jar salsa	.5 kg
¼ cup sour cream	60 ml
1 tablespoon flour	15 ml
3 tablespoons snipped fresh cilantro	45 ml
1 (8 ounce) package shredded 4-cheese blend	227 g

- Cut tortillas into 6 wedges. In sprayed slow cooker, place half of tortillas wedges.

- Place remaining wedges on baking pan, bake about 10 minutes at 250° (121° C) and set aside.

- Layer chicken, corn and beans over tortillas in cooker.

- In bowl combine salsa, sour cream, flour and cilantro and pour over corn and beans.

- Cover and cook on LOW for 3 to 4 hours.

- When ready to serve, place baked tortillas wedges on top of each serving. Serves 4 to 6.

Chicken and Stuffing

1 (10 ounce) can cream of chicken soup	280 g
2 stalks celery, sliced	
½ cup (1 stick) butter, melted	120 ml
3 cups cooked, cubed chicken	710 ml
1 (16 ounce) package frozen broccoli, corn and red peppers	.5 kg
1 (8 ounce) box cornbread stuffing mix	227 g

- In large mixing bowl, combine chicken soup, celery, butter, chicken, vegetables, stuffing mix and ⅓ cup (80 ml) water. Mix well and transfer to 5 or 6-quart (5 L) slow cooker.

- Cover and cook on LOW for 5 to 6 hours. Serves 4 to 6.

TIP: This is a great recipe for leftover chicken.

Chicken and Everything Good

2 (10 ounce) cans cream of chicken soup	2 (280 g)
⅓ cup (⅔ stick) butter, melted	80 ml
3 cups cooked, cubed chicken	710 ml
1 (16 ounce) package frozen broccoli, corn and red peppers	.5 kg
1 (10 ounce) package frozen green peas	280 g
1 (8 ounce) package cornbread stuffing mix	227 g

- Spray, large slow cooker. In mixing bowl, combine soup, melted butter and 1/3 cup (80 ml) water and mix well. Add chicken, vegetables and stuffing mix and stir well. Spoon mixture into cooker. Cover and cook on LOW for 5 to 6 hours or on HIGH for 2 hours 30 minutes to 3 hours.
Serves 4 to 6.

Chicken Alfredo

1½ pounds boneless, skinless chicken thighs, cut into strips	.7 kg
2 ribs celery, sliced diagonally	
1 sweet red bell pepper, cored, seeded, julienned	
1 (16 ounce) jar alfredo sauce	.5 kg
3 cups fresh broccoli florets	710 ml
1 (8 ounce) package fettuccine or linguine	227 g
1 (4 ounce) package shredded parmesan cheese	114 g

- Cut chicken into strips.

- In sprayed 4 to 5-quart (4 L) slow cooker, layer chicken, celery and bell pepper.

- Pour alfredo sauce evenly over vegetables.

- Cover and cook on LOW for 5 to 6 hours.

- About 30 minutes before serving, turn heat to HIGH and add broccoli florets to chicken-alfredo mixture.

- Cover and cook additional 30 minutes.

- Cook pasta according to package directions and drain.

- Just before serving pour pasta into cooker, mix and sprinkle parmesan cheese on top. Serves 4 to 6.

Sweet and Spicy Chicken

2 pounds chicken thighs	1 kg
¾ cup chili sauce	180 ml
¾ cup packed brown sugar	180 ml
1 (1 ounce) packet dry onion soup mix	28 g
⊠ teaspoon cayenne pepper	.5 ml

- Spray 5-quart (5 L) slow cooker and arrange chicken pieces in bottom of cooker. Combine chili sauce, brown sugar, dry onion soup mix, cayenne pepper and ¼ cup (60 ml) water and spoon over chicken.

- Cover and cook on LOW for 6 to 7 hours. Serve over hot, cooked rice. Serves 4 to 6.

Maple-Plum Glazed Turkey Breast

1 cup red plum jam	240 ml
1 cup maple syrup	240 ml
1 teaspoon dry mustard	5 ml
¼ cup lemon juice	60 ml
1 (3 - 5 pound) bone-in turkey breast	1.3 kg

- In saucepan, combine jam, syrup, mustard and lemon juice. Bring to a boil, turn heat down and simmer about 20 minutes or until slightly thick. Reserve 1 cup (240 ml).

- Place turkey breast in slow cooker and pour remaining glaze over turkey. Cover and cook on LOW for 5 to 7 hours.

- When ready to serve, slice turkey and serve with heated, reserved glaze. Serves 6 to 8.

Southern Chicken

1 cup half-and-half cream	240 ml
1 tablespoon flour	15 ml
1 (1 ounce) packet chicken gravy mix	28 g
1 pound boneless, skinless chicken thighs	.5 kg
1 (16 ounce) package frozen stew vegetables, thawed	.5 kg
1 (4 ounce) jar sliced mushrooms, drained	114 g
1 (10 ounce) package frozen green peas, thawed	280 g
1½ cups biscuit baking mix	360 ml
1 bunch fresh green onions, chopped	
½ cup milk	120 ml

- In bowl, combine cream, flour, gravy mix and 1 cup (240 ml) water, stir until smooth and pour in large slow cooker.

- Cut chicken into 1-inch (2.5 cm) pieces and stir in vegetables and mushrooms.

- Cover and cook on LOW for 4 to 6 hours or until chicken is tender and sauce thickens. Stir in peas.

- In bowl, combine baking mix, onions and milk and mix well.

- Drop dough by tablespoonfuls onto chicken mixture.

- Change heat to HIGH, cover and cook additional 50 to 60 minutes. Serves 4 to 6.

Italian Chicken

1 small head cabbage	
1 onion	
1 (4 ounce) jar sliced mushrooms, drained	**114 g**
1 medium zucchini, sliced	
1 sweet red bell pepper, cored, seeded, julienned	
1 teaspoon Italian seasoning	**5 ml**
1½ pounds boneless, skinless chicken thighs	**.7 kg**
2 (15 ounce) cans Italian stewed tomatoes	**2 (425 g)**
1 teaspoon minced garlic	**5 ml**

- Spray 6-quart slow cooker.

- Cut cabbage into wedges, slice onions and separate into rings.

- Make layers of cabbage, mushrooms, onion, zucchini and bell pepper in cooker.

- Sprinkle Italian seasoning over vegetables. Place chicken thighs on top of vegetables.

- Mix garlic with tomatoes and pour over chicken.

- Cover and cook on LOW for 4 to 6 hours. Serves 4 to 6.

TIP: When serving, sprinkle a little parmesan cheese over each serving.

Asparagus-Cheese Chicken

8 - 10 boneless, skinless chicken thighs	
2 tablespoons butter	30 ml
1 (10 ounce) can cream of celery soup	280 g
1 (10 ounce) can cheddar cheese soup	280 g
⅓ cup milk	80 ml
1 (16 ounce) package frozen asparagus cuts	.5 kg

- Place chicken thighs in sprayed 5-quart (5 L) slow cooker.

- In saucepan, combine butter, celery soup, cheddar cheese soup and milk. Heat just enough for butter to melt and mix well. Pour over chicken thighs.

- Cover and cook on LOW for 5 to 6 hours. Remove cover and place asparagus cuts over chicken and cook additional 1 hour. Serves 4 to 6.

Arroz Con Pollo

3 pounds chicken thighs	
2 (15 ounce) cans Italian stewed tomatoes	2 (425 g)
1 (16 ounce) package frozen green peas, thawed	.5 kg
2 cups long grain rice	480 ml
1 (.28 ounce) packet yellow rice seasoning mix	8 g
2 (14 ounce) cans chicken broth	2 (396 g)
1 heaping teaspoon minced garlic	5 ml
1 teaspoon dried oregano	5 ml

- In large, sprayed slow cooker, combine all ingredients plus ¾ cup (180 ml) water and stir well.

- Cover and cook on LOW for 7 to 8 hours or on HIGH for 3 hours 30 minutes to 4 hours. Serves 6 to 8.

Turkey Bake

1½ pounds turkey tenderloins	.7 kg
1 (6 ounce) package Oriental rice and vermicelli	168 g
1 (10 ounce) package frozen green peas, thawed	280 g
1 cup sliced celery	240 ml
¼ cup (½ stick) butter, melted	60 ml
1 (14 ounce) can chicken broth	396 g
1½ cups fresh broccoli florets	360 ml

- Cut tenderloins into strips. In non-stick skillet, saute turkey strips until it is no longer pink.

- In large slow cooker, combine turkey strips, rice-vermicelli mix plus seasoning packet, peas, celery, butter, chicken broth and 1 cup (240 ml) water and mix well.

- Cover and cook on LOW for 4 to 5 hours. Turn heat to HIGH setting, add broccoli and cook additional 20 minutes. Serves 4 to 6.

Turkey Cassoulet

2 cups cooked, cubed turkey	**480 ml**
1 (8 ounce) package smoked turkey sausage	**227 g**
3 carrots, sliced	
1 onion, halved, sliced	
1 (15 ounce) can navy bean	**425 g**
1 (15 ounce) can white lima beans	**425 g**
1 (8 ounce) can tomato sauce	**227 g**
1 teaspoon dried thyme	**5 ml**
¼ teaspoon ground allspice	**1 ml**

- Cut turkey sausage in ½-inch (1.2 cm) pieces.

- Combine all ingredients in sprayed slow cooker.

- Cover and cook on LOW for 4 to 5 hours. Serves 4.

TIP: This is a great recipe for leftover turkey

Tangy Chicken Legs

12 - 15 chicken legs	
⅓ cup soy sauce	**80 ml**
⅔ cup packed brown sugar	**160 ml**
Scant ⅛ teaspoon ground ginger	**.5 ml**

- Place chicken legs in sprayed 5-quart (5 L) slow cooker.

- Combine soy sauce, brown sugar, ¼ cup (60 ml) water and ginger and spoon over chicken legs.

- Cover and cook on LOW for 4 to 5 hours. Serves 6 to 8.

Turkey Loaf

2 pounds ground turkey	**1 kg**
1 onion, very finely chopped	
½ sweet red bell pepper, very finely chopped	
2 teaspoons minced garlic	**10 ml**
½ cup chili sauce	**120 ml**
2 large eggs, beaten	
¾ cup Italian seasoned breadcrumbs	**180 ml**

- Make foil handles by cutting 3 (3 x 18-inch/8 x 45 cm) strips of heavy foil; place in bottom of slow cooker in crisscross strips (resembles spokes on wheel) up and over sides.

- In large bowl, combine all ingredients plus 1 teaspoon (5 ml) salt and ½ teaspoon (2 ml) pepper and mix well.

- Shape into round loaf and place on top foil. Fold extended strips over food. When finished cooking, lift food out by handles.

- Cover and cook on LOW for 5 to 6 hours. Serves 4 to 6.

Turkey Spaghetti

2 pounds ground turkey	1 kg
2 (10 ounce) cans tomato-bisque soup	2 (280 g)
1 (14 ounce) can chicken broth	396 g
2 (7 ounce) boxes ready-cut spaghetti, cooked, drained	2 (198 g)
1 (15 ounce) can whole kernel corn, drained	425 g
1 (4 ounce) can sliced mushrooms, drained	114 g
¼ cup ketchup	60 ml

- In non-stick skillet, cook ground turkey and season with a little salt and pepper. Place cooked turkey in 5 to 6-quart (5 L) slow cooker. Add in soups, spaghetti, corn and mushrooms and stir to blend.

- Cover and cook on LOW for 5 to 7 hours or on HIGH for 3 hours. Serves 4 to 6.

Colorful Rice and Turkey

1 (10 ounce) can cream of mushroom	280 g
1 (10 ounce) can cream of chicken soup	280 g
2 cups white rice	480 ml
3 ribs celery, sliced diagonally	
1 (16 ounce) package frozen Oriental vegetable mix	.5 kg
3 cups cooked, cubed turkey (or chicken)	710 ml
1 teaspoon poultry seasoning	5 ml
2 (14 ounce) cans chicken broth	2 (396 g)

- Pour mushroom soup and chicken soup in saucepan and add 1 soup can water. Heat just enough to mix well and pour into sprayed 5 to 6-quart (5 L) slow cooker.

- Add all other ingredients and mix. Cover and cook on LOW for 5 to 6 hours.
Serves 4 to 6.

Sausage and Rice

1 pound turkey sausage	.5 kg
1 (6 ounce) box flavored rice mix	168 g
2 (14 ounce) cans chicken broth	2 (396 g)
2 cups sliced celery	480 ml
1 sweet red bell pepper, cored, seeded, julienned	
1 (15 ounce) can cut green beans, drained	425 g
⅓ cup slivered almonds, toasted	80 ml

- Break up turkey sausage and brown in skillet.

- Place in sprayed 4 to 5-quart (4 L) slow cooker.

- Add rice, 1 cup (240 ml) water, chicken broth, celery, bell pepper and green beans and stir to mix.

- Cover and cook on LOW for 3 to 4 hours.

- When ready to serve, sprinkle almonds over top. Serves 4.

BEEF

Savory Steak

Great sauce with mashed potatoes

1½ pounds lean round steak	**.7 kg**
1 onion, halved, sliced	
2 (10 ounce) cans golden mushroom soup	**2 (280 g)**
1½ cups hot, thick-and-chunky salsa	**360 ml**

- Trim fat from steak and cut into serving-size pieces.

- Sprinkle with 1 teaspoon (5 ml) pepper and place in sprayed 5 to 6-quart (6 L) slow cooker.

- Place onion slices over steak.

- Combine mushroom soup and salsa and mix well. Spoon over steak and onions.

- Cover and cook on LOW for 7 to 8 hours. Serves 4 to 6.

Pepper Steak

1½ pounds round steak	.7 kg
¼ cup soy sauce	60 ml
1 onion, sliced	
1 teaspoon minced garlic	5 ml
1 teaspoon sugar	5 ml
¼ teaspoon ground ginger	1 ml
1 (15 ounce) can stewed tomatoes	425 g
2 green bell peppers, cored, seeded, julienned	
1 teaspoon beef bouillon granules	5 ml
1 tablespoon cornstarch	15 ml

- Slice beef in strips, brown in skillet with a little oil and place in oval slow cooker.

- Combine soy sauce, onion, garlic, sugar and ginger in bowl and pour over beef.

- Cover and cook on LOW for 5 to 6 hours.

- Add tomatoes, green peppers and bouillon and cook 1 hour more.

- Combine cornstarch and ¼ cup water (60 ml) in cup and stir into cooker. Continue cooking until liquid thickens.

- Serve over hot, buttered rice or noodles.
  Serves 4 to 6.

Swiss Steak

1 - 1½ pounds boneless, round steak	**.5 kg**
½ teaspoon seasoned salt	**2 ml**
½ teaspoon seasoned pepper	**2 ml**
8 - 10 medium new potatoes with peels, halved	
1 cup baby carrots	**240 ml**
1 onion, sliced	
1 (15 ounce) can stewed tomatoes	**425 g**
1 (12 ounce) jar beef gravy	**340 g**

- Cut steak in 6 to 8 serving-size pieces, season with seasoned salt and pepper and brown in non-stick skillet.

- Layer steak pieces, potatoes, carrots and onion in slow cooker.

- In bowl, combine tomatoes and beef gravy and spoon over vegetables.

- Cover and cook on LOW for 7 to 8 hours. Serves 4 to 6.

Spicy Swiss Steak

1½ pounds boneless, beef round steak	**.7 kg**
4 ounces spicy bratwurst	**114 g**
2 small onions	
2 tablespoons quick-cooking tapioca	**30 ml**
1 teaspoon dried thyme	**5 ml**
2 (15 ounce) cans Mexican stewed tomatoes	**2 (425 g)**

- Trim fat from steak and cut into 4 serving-size pieces.

- In skillet, brown steak and bratwurst. Drain and place in sprayed 4 to 5-quart (5 L) slow cooker.

- Slice onions and separate into rings.

- Cover meat with onions and sprinkle with tapioca, thyme, a little salt and pepper. Pour stewed tomatoes over onion and seasonings.

- Cover and cook on LOW for 5 to 8 hours.

- Serve over hot, cooked noodles. Serves 4 to 6.

Stroganoff

2 pounds beef round steak	1 kg
¾ cup flour, divided	180 ml
½ teaspoon mustard	2 ml
2 onions, thinly sliced	
½ pound fresh mushrooms, sliced	227 g
1 (10 ounce) can beef broth	280 g
¼ cup dry white wine or cooking wine	60 ml
1 (8 ounce) carton sour cream	227 g

- Trim excess fat from steak and cut into 3-inch (8 cm) strips about ½-inch (1.2 cm) wide. In bowl, combine ½ cup (120 ml) flour, mustard and a little salt and pepper and toss with steak strips.

- Place strips in sprayed, oval slow cooker.

- Cover with onions and mushrooms. Add beef broth and wine. Cover and cook on LOW for 8 to 10 hours.

- Just before serving, combine sour cream and ¼ cup (60 ml) flour in bowl.

- Stir into cooker and cook additional 10 to 15 minutes or until stroganoff thickens slightly. Serves 4 to 6.

Teriyaki Steak

1½ - 2 pounds flank steak	.7 kg
1 (15 ounce) can sliced pineapple with juice	425 g
1 tablespoon white wine Worcestershire sauce	15 ml
⅓ cup packed brown sugar	80 ml
3 tablespoons soy sauce	45 ml
½ teaspoon ground ginger	2 ml
1 (14 ounce) can chicken broth	396 g
1 cup long grain converted rice	240 ml

- Roll flank steak, tie and cut into 7 to 8 individual steaks.

- In bowl large enough for marinade to cover individual steaks, combine ½ cup (120 ml) pineapple juice, Worcestershire, sugar, soy sauce and ginger.

- Add steak rolls and marinate for 1 hour in sauce.

- Pour chicken broth into sprayed slow cooker.

- Add rice and ¾ cup (180 ml) water. Place steaks over rice and broth.

- Cover and cook on LOW for 8 to 10 hours. Serves 4 to 6.

Mushroom-Round Steak

1½ - 2 pounds round steak	**.7 kg**
1 (1 ounce) packet dry onion soup mix	**28 g**
½ cup dry red wine	**120 ml**
1 (8 ounce) carton fresh mushrooms, sliced	**227 g**
1 (10 ounce) can French onion soup	**280 g**

- Cut round steak in serving-size pieces and place in sprayed, oval slow cooker.

- Combine soup mix, red wine, mushrooms, French onion soup and ½ cup (120 ml) water; spoon over steak pieces.

- Cover and cook on LOW for 7 to 8 hours. Serves 4 to 6.

O'Brian's Hash

3 cups cooked, cubed beef roast	**710 ml**
1 (28 ounce) package frozen hashbrowns with	
onions and peppers, thawed	**794 g**
1 (16 ounce) jar salsa	**.5 kg**
1 tablespoon beef seasoning	**15 ml**
1 cup shredded cheddar-Jack cheese	**240 ml**

- Place beef in large, sprayed slow cooker.

- Brown potatoes in little oil in large skillet. Stir in salsa and beef seasoning and transfer to slow cooker.

- Cover and cook on HIGH for 4 to 5 hours.

- When ready to serve, sprinkle cheese over top. Serves 4.

Italian Steak

1 pound round steak, cubed	.5 kg
2 cups fresh mushroom halves	480 ml
1 (15 ounce) can Italian stewed tomatoes	425 g
1 (10 ounce) can beef broth	280 g
½ cup red wine	120 ml
2 teaspoons Italian seasoning	10 ml
3 tablespoons quick-cooking tapioca	45 ml

- Place beef in sprayed 4 to 5-quart (5 L) slow cooker.

- Combine mushrooms, tomatoes, beef broth, wine, Italian seasoning, tapioca and a little salt and pepper. Pour over steak.

- Cover and cook on LOW for 8 to 10 hours.

- Serve over hot, buttered linguine. Serves 4.

Beefy Onion Supper

1 - 1½ pounds round steak	.5 kg
1 onion	
2 cups fresh sliced mushrooms	480 ml
1 (10 ounce) can French onion soup	280 g
1 (6 ounce) package herb stuffing mix	168 g
½ cup (1 stick) butter, melted	120 ml

- Cut beef into 5 to 6 serving-size pieces.

- Slice onion and separate into rings.

- In oval slow cooker, place steak pieces and top with mushrooms and onions.

- Pour soup over ingredients in cooker.

- Cover and cook on LOW for 7 to 9 hours.

- Just before serving, combine stuffing mix with seasoning packet, butter and ½ cup (120 ml) liquid from cooker and toss to mix.

- Place stuffing mixture on top of steak and increase heat to HIGH.

- Cover and cook additional 15 minutes or until stuffing is fluffy. Serves 4 to 6.

Beef Roulades

1½ pounds beef flank steak	.7 kg
5 slices bacon	
¾ cup finely chopped onion	180 ml
1 (4 ounce) can mushrooms pieces	114 g
1 tablespoon Worcestershire sauce	15 ml
⅓ cup Italian-seasoned breadcrumbs	80 ml
1 (12 ounce) jar beef gravy	340 g

- Cut steak into 4 to 6 serving-size pieces. With kitchen shears, cut bacon into small pieces and combine with onion, mushrooms, Worcestershire and breadcrumbs. Place about ½ cup (120 ml) onion mixture on each piece of steak.

- Roll meat and secure ends with wooden toothpicks. Dry beef rolls with paper towels. In skillet, brown steak rolls and transfer to sprayed slow cooker.

- Pour gravy evenly over steaks to thoroughly moisten. Cover and cook on LOW for 7 to 9 hours. Serves 4 to 6.

TIP: This is really good served with mashed potatoes. Have you tried instant mashed potatoes as a time-saver?

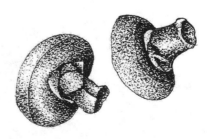

Beef Tips Over Noodles

½ cup plus 3 tablespoons flour, divided	120 ml/ 45 ml
3 pounds beef tips	1.3 kg
1 (8 ounce) carton fresh mushrooms, sliced	227 g
1 bunch fresh green onions, chopped	
1 small sweet red bell pepper, chopped	
¼ cup ketchup	60 ml
1 (14 ounce) can beef broth	396 g
1 tablespoon Worcestershire sauce	15 ml

- In bowl, coat beef tips with ½ cup (120 ml) flour and transfer to sprayed slow cooker.

- Add mushrooms, onion, bell pepper, ketchup, broth, Worcestershire sauce and a little salt and pepper.

- Cover and cook on LOW for 8 to 9 hours.
  About 1 hour before serving, turn heat to HIGH.

- In small bowl, combine remaining flour with ¼ cup (60 ml) water, stir into cooker and cook until liquid thickens.

- Serve over hot, buttered noodles. Serves 6 to 8.

Beef Tips Over Pasta

2 - 2½ pounds lean, beef stew meat	1 kg
2 cups frozen, small whole onions, thawed	480 ml
1 green bell pepper, seeded	
1 (6 ounce) jar pitted Greek olives or ripe olives	168 g
½ cup sun-dried tomatoes in oil, drained, chopped	120 ml
1 (28 ounce) jar marinara sauce	794 g
1 (8 ounce) package pasta twirls	227 g

- In sprayed 4 or 5-quart (5 L) slow cooker, place beef and onions.

- Cut bell pepper in 1-inch (2.5 cm) cubes and add to slow cooker.

- Add olives, tomatoes and bell pepper and pour marinara sauce over top.

- Cover and cook on LOW for 8 to 10 hours.

- Serve over hot, cooked pasta twirls. Serves 4 to 6.

Pot Roast and Veggies

1 (2 pound) chuck roast	1 kg
4 - 5 medium potatoes, peeled, quartered	
4 large carrots, quartered	
1 onion, quartered	
1 (14 ounce) can beef broth	396 g
2 tablespoons cornstarch	30 ml

- Trim fat from pieces of roast. Cut roast into 2 equal pieces.

- In skillet, brown pieces of roast. (Coat pieces with flour, salt and pepper if you'd like a little "breading" on the outside.) Spray 4 to 5-quart (4 L) slow cooker.

- Place potatoes, carrots and onion in slow cooker and mix well. Place browned beef over vegetables.

- Pour 1½ cups (360 ml) broth over beef and vegetables. Save remaining broth and chill.

- Cover and cook on LOW for 8 to 9 hours. About 5 minutes before serving, remove beef and vegetables with slotted spoon and place on serving platter. Cover to keep warm.

- Pour liquid from slow cooker into medium saucepan.

- In bowl, blend remaining ½ cup (120 ml) broth and cornstarch until smooth and add to liquid in saucepan. Boil 1 minute and stir constantly.

- Serve gravy with roast and veggies and season with a little salt and pepper, if desired. Serves 4 to 6.

Sweet-and-Sour Beef

1 (2 pound) boneless chuck roast	1 kg
½ cup flour	120 ml
Oil	
1 onion, sliced	
½ cup chili sauce	120 ml
¾ cup packed brown sugar	180 ml
¼ cup red wine vinegar	60 ml
1 tablespoon Worcestershire sauce	15 ml
1 (16 ounce) package baby carrots	.5 kg

- Cut beef into 1-inch cubes and dredge in flour and a little salt and pepper.

- In skillet, brown beef in a little oil and place in sprayed slow cooker.

- Add remaining ingredients, except carrots, and 1 cup (240 ml) water.

- Cover and cook on LOW for 7 to 8 hours.

- Add carrots and cook 1 hour 30 minutes. Serves 4 to 6.

Old-Time Pot Roast

1 (2 - 2½) pound boneless rump roast	1 kg
5 medium potatoes, peeled, quartered	
1 (16 ounce) package peeled baby carrots	.5 kg
2 medium onions, quartered	
1 (10 ounce) can golden mushroom soup	280 g
½ teaspoon dried basil	2 ml
½ teaspoon seasoned salt	2 ml

- Brown roast on all sides in large, non-stick skillet.

- Place potatoes, carrots and onions in sprayed 4 to 5-quart (4 L) slow cooker.

- Place browned roast on top of vegetables.

- In bowl, combine soup, basil and seasoned salt and pour mixture over meat and vegetables.

- Cover and cook on LOW for 9 to 11 hours. Serves 4 to 6.

TIP: To serve, transfer roast and vegetables to serving plate. Stir juices remaining in slow cooker and spoon over roast and vegetables.

Beef Tips and Mushrooms Supreme

2 (10 ounce) cans golden mushroom soup	2 (280 g)
1 (14 ounce) can beef broth	396 g
1 tablespoon beef seasoning	15 ml
2 (4 ounce) cans sliced mushrooms, drained	2 (114 g)
2 pounds round steak	1 kg
Hot buttered noodles	
1 (8 ounce) carton sour cream	227 g

- Combine both cans of mushroom soup, beef broth, beef seasoning and sliced mushrooms. Place in slow cooker and stir to blend.

- Add slices of beef and stir well.

- Cover and cook on LOW for 4 to 5 hours.

- When ready to serve, cook noodles, drain, add salt and a little butter.

- Stir sour cream into sauce in slow cooker. Spoon sauce and beef over noodles. Serves 4 to 6.

Herb-Crusted Beef Roast

1 (2 - 3 pound) beef rump roast	1 kg
¼ cup chopped fresh parsley	60 ml
¼ cup chopped fresh oregano leaves	60 ml
½ teaspoon dried rosemary leaves	2 ml
1 teaspoon minced garlic	5 ml
1 tablespoon oil	15 ml
6 slices thick-cut bacon	

- Rub roast with a little salt and pepper.

- In small bowl, combine parsley, oregano, rosemary, garlic and oil and press mixture on top and sides of roast.

- Place roast in slow cooker. Place bacon over top of beef and tuck ends under bottom.

- Cover and cook on LOW for 6 to 8 hours. Serves 4 to 6.

Cola Roast

1 (4 pound) chuck roast	1.8 kg
1 (12 ounce) bottle chili sauce	340 g
1 onion, chopped	
1 (12 ounce) can cola	340 g
1 tablespoon Worcestershire sauce	15 ml

- Score roast in several places and fill each slit with a little salt and pepper.

- In skillet, sear roast on all sides. Place in 5-quart (5 L) slow cooker.

- Combine chili sauce, chopped onion, cola and Worcestershire and mix well. Pour over roast.

- Cover and cook on LOW for 8 to 9 hours. Serves 6 to 8.

Classic Beef Roast

1 (3 - 4 pound) beef chuck roast	1.3 kg
1 (1 ounce) packet dry onion soup mix	28 g
2 (10 ounce) cans golden onion soup	2 (280 g)
3 - 4 medium potatoes, quartered	

- Place roast in large, sprayed slow cooker.

- Sprinkle soup mix on roast and spoon on condensed soup. Place potatoes around roast.

- Cover and cook on LOW for 7 to 8 hours or on HIGH for 4 hours. Serves 6 to 8.

Mushroom Beef

1 (10 ounce) can beefy mushroom soup	280 g
1 (10 ounce) can golden mushroom soup	280 g
1 (10 ounce) can French onion soup	280 g
⅓ cup seasoned breadcrumbs	80 ml
2½ pounds lean beef stew meat	1.2 kg
Hot buttered noodles	

- In 6-quart (6 L) slow cooker combine soups, ½ teaspoon (2 ml) pepper, breadcrumbs and ¾ cup (180 ml) water. Stir in beef cubes and mix well.

- Cover and cook on LOW for 8 to 9 hours.

- Serve over hot, buttered noodles. Serves 6 to 8.

Sweet and Savory Brisket

1 (3 - 4 pound) trimmed beef brisket, halved	1.3 kg
⅓ cup grape or plum jelly	80 ml
1 cup ketchup	240 ml
1 (1 ounce) packet dry onion soup mix	28 g

- Place half of brisket in slow cooker.

- In saucepan, combine jelly, ketchup, onion soup mix and ¾ teaspoon (4 ml) pepper and heat just enough to mix well. Spread half over brisket.

- Top with remaining brisket and jelly-soup mixture.

- Cover and cook on LOW for 8 to 9 hours. Slice brisket and serve with cooking juices. Serves 6 to 8.

Beef Roast

1 (4 pound) boneless rump roast	1.8 kg
½ cup flour, divided	120 ml
1 (1 ounce) packet brown gravy mix	28 g
1 (1 ounce) packet beefy onion soup mix	28 g

- Spray 5 to 6-quart (5 L) slow cooker and cut roast in half (if needed to fit into cooker).

- Place roast in cooker and rub half of flour over roast.

- In small bowl, combine remaining flour, gravy mix and soup mix, gradually add 2 cups (480 ml) water and stir until they mix well. Pour over roast.

- Cover and cook on LOW for 7 to 8 hours or until roast is tender. Serves 6 to 8.

TIP: This is a great gravy to serve over mashed potatoes. Use instant mashed potatoes. They will never know the difference and will love the meal!

Smoked Brisket

1 (4 - 6 pound) trimmed brisket	1.8 kg
1 (4 ounce) bottle liquid smoke	114 g
Garlic salt	
Celery salt	
Worcestershire sauce	
1 onion, chopped	
1 (6 ounce) bottle barbecue sauce	168 g

- Place brisket in large shallow dish and pour liquid smoke over top.

- Sprinkle with garlic salt and celery salt. Cover and chill overnight.

- Before cooking, drain liquid smoke and douse brisket with Worcestershire sauce.

- Place chopped onion in slow cooker and place brisket on top of onion.

- Cover and cook on LOW for 7 to 9 hours.

- With 1 hour left on cooking time, pour barbecue sauce over brisket and cook 1 hour. Serves 6 to 8.

Good Brisket

½ cup packed brown sugar	120 ml
1 tablespoon Cajun seasoning	15 ml
2 teaspoons lemon pepper	10 ml
1 tablespoon Worcestershire sauce	15 ml
1 (3 - 4 pound) trimmed beef brisket	1.3 kg

- In small bowl, combine sugar, seasoning, lemon pepper and Worcestershire and spread on brisket.

- Place brisket in sprayed, oval slow cooker.

- Cover and cook on LOW for 6 to 8 hours. Serves 6 to 8.

Meat and Potatoes

4 medium potatoes, peeled, sliced	
1¼ pounds lean ground beef, browned	567 g
1 onion, sliced	
1 (10 ounce) can cream of mushroom soup	280 g
1 (10 ounce) can vegetable beef soup	280 g

- In large slow cooker, layer all ingredients with a little salt and pepper.

- Cover and cook on LOW for 5 to 6 hours. Serves 4 to 6.

Brisket and Gravy

1 (3 - 4 pound) trimmed beef brisket	1.3 kg
¼ cup chili sauce	60 ml
1 (1 ounce) packet herb-garlic soup mix	28 g
2 tablespoons Worcestershire sauce	30 ml
3 tablespoons cornstarch	45 ml

- Place beef brisket in sprayed 5 to 6-quart (5 L) slow cooker. Cut to fit if necessary.

- In bowl, combine chili sauce, soup mix, Worcestershire and 1½ cups (360 ml) water and pour over brisket.

- Cover and cook on LOW for 9 to 11 hours.

- Remove brisket and keep warm. Pour juices into 2-cup (480 ml) glass measuring cup and skim fat.

- In saucepan stir cornstarch and ¼ cup (60 ml) water. Add 1½ cups (360 ml) juices and cook, while stirring constantly, until gravy thickens.

- Slice beef thinly across grain and serve with mashed potatoes and gravy. Serves 6 to 8.

Shredded Brisket for Sandwiches

2 teaspoons onion powder	10 ml
1 teaspoon minced garlic	5 ml
1 (3 - 4 pound) beef brisket	1.3 kg
1 tablespoon liquid smoke	15 ml
1 (16 ounce) bottle barbecue sauce	.5 kg

- Combine onion powder, minced garlic and liquid smoke and rub over brisket.

- Place brisket in large, sprayed slow cooker. Add ⅓ cup (80 ml) water to cooker.

- Cover and cook on LOW for 6 to 8 hours or until brisket is tender.

- Remove brisket, cool and reserve ½ cup (120 ml) cooking juices.

- Shred brisket with 2 forks and place in large saucepan. Add ½ cup (120 ml) cooking juices and barbecue sauce and heat thoroughly.

- Make sandwiches with kaiser rolls or hamburger buns. Serves 6 to 8.

219

A Different Corned Beef

2 onions, sliced
Lemon pepper
1 (3 - 4 pound) seasoned corned beef   **1.3 kg**

- Place sliced onions in large slow cooker. Add 1 cup (240 ml) water. Sprinkle lemon pepper liberally over corned beef and place on top on onion. Cover and cook on LOW for 7 to 9 hours.

- Remove corned beef from slow cooker and place in ovenproof pan. Preheat oven to 375° (190° C).

Glaze:
¼ cup honey   **60 ml**
¼ cup frozen orange juice concentrate, thawed   **60 ml**
1 tablespoon mustard   **15 ml**

- Prepare glaze by combining all ingredients and spoon over corned beef. Bake for 30 minutes and baste occasionally with glaze before serving. Serves 6 to 8.

Beef Ribs and Gravy

4 pounds beef short ribs	**2 kg**
1 onion, sliced	
1 (12 ounce) jar beef gravy	**340 g**
1 (1 ounce) packet beef gravy mix	**28 g**

- Spray 6-quart (6 L) slow cooker and place beef ribs inside. Cover with onion and sprinkle with 1 teaspoon (5 ml) pepper. In small bowl, combine beef gravy and dry gravy mix and pour over ribs and onion.

- Cover and cook on LOW for 9 to 11 hours. (The ribs must cook this long on LOW to tenderize.) Serves 4 to 6.

TIP: Serve with hot mashed potatoes and gravy.

Beef and Noodles al Grande

1½ pounds lean ground beef	.7 kg
1 (16 ounce) package frozen onions and	
bell peppers, thawed	.5 kg
1 (16 ounce) box cubed Velveeta® cheese	.5 kg
2 (15 ounce) cans Mexican stewed tomatoes	
with liquid	425 g
2 (15 ounce) cans whole kernel corn, drained	2 (425 g)
1 (8 ounce) package medium egg noodles	227 g
1 cup shredded cheddar cheese	240 ml

- In skillet, brown ground beef and drain fat.

- Place beef in sprayed 5 to 6-quart (5 L) slow cooker, add onions and peppers, cheese, tomatoes, corn and about 1 teaspoon (5 ml) salt and mix well.

- Cover and cook on LOW for 4 to 5 hours.

- Cook noodles according to package direction, drain and fold into beef-tomato mixture. Cook additional 30 minutes to heat thoroughly.

- When ready to serve, top with cheddar cheese, several sprinkles of chopped fresh parsley or chopped fresh green onions. Serves 4 to 6.

Stuffed Cabbage

10 - 12 large cabbage leaves	
1½ pounds lean ground beef	.7 kg
½ cup brown rice	120 ml
1 egg, beaten	
¼ teaspoon ground cinnamon	1 ml
1 (15 ounce) can tomato sauce	425 g

- Wash cabbage leaves, place in saucepan of boiling water and turn off heat. Soak about 5 minutes.

- Remove leaves, drain and cool.

- In bowl, combine beef, rice, egg, 1 teaspoon (5 ml) salt, ½ teaspoon (2 ml) pepper, cinnamon and mix well.

- Place 2 tablespoons (30 ml) beef mixture on each cabbage leaf and roll tightly. (If you can't get 10 to 12 large leaves, put 2 together to make 1 large leaf.)

- Stack rolls in sprayed, oval slow cooker and pour tomato sauce over rolls.

- Cover and cook on HIGH for 1 hour, lower heat to LOW and cook additional 6 to 7 hours. Serves 4 to 6.

Southwest Spaghetti

1½ pounds lean ground beef	.7 kg
2½ teaspoons chili powder	12 ml
1 (15 ounce) can tomato sauce	425 g
1 (7 ounce) package spaghetti	198 g
1 heaping tablespoon beef seasoning	15 ml
Shredded cheddar-Jack cheese	

- In skillet, brown ground beef until no longer pink. Place in 4 to 5-quart (5 L) slow cooker. Add chili powder, tomato sauce, spaghetti, 2⅓ cups (560 ml) water and beef seasoning and mix well.

- Cover and cook on LOW for 6 to 7 hours.

- When ready to serve, cover with lots of shredded cheddar-Jack cheese. Serves 4 to 6.

Beef and Gravy

2 pounds sirloin steak or thick round steak	1 kg
Oil	
1 (1 ounce) packet dry onion soup mix	28 g
1 (10 ounce) can golden mushroom soup	280 g
1 (4 ounce) can sliced mushrooms, drained	114 g
Hot buttered noodles	

- Cut Steak in ½-inch (1.2cm) pieces. Brown beef in skillet in a little oil and place in 5 to 6 quart (5 L) slow cooker.

- Combine onion soup mix, mushroom soup, mushrooms and ½ cup (120 ml) water and mix well. Spoon over top of beef.

- Cover and cook on LOW for 7 to 8 hours. Serve over hot, cooked noodles. Serves 4 to 6.

Sauce for Fancy Meatballs

1 (16 ounce) can whole-berry cranberry sauce	.5 kg
1 cup ketchup	240 ml
⅓ cup packed brown sugar	160 ml
½ cup beef broth	120 ml
1 (18 ounce) package frozen meatballs, thawed	510 g

- Combine cranberry sauce, ketchup, brown sugar and broth in large slow cooker.

- Turn heat to HIGH and let mixture come to a boil for 30 minutes to 1 hour. Place package of thawed meatballs in sauce.

- Cover and cook on LOW for 2 hours.

- Remove meatballs to serving dish with slotted spoon. Insert toothpicks for easy pick up.

- Serve as an appetizer, for supper or buffet pick-up food. Serves 4 to 6.

Make-Believe Lasagna

1 pound lean ground beef	.5 kg
1 onion, chopped	
½ teaspoon garlic powder	2 ml
1 (18 ounce) can spaghetti sauce	510 g
½ teaspoon ground oregano	2 ml
6 - 8 lasagna noodles, divided	
1 (12 ounce) carton cottage cheese, divided	340 g
½ cup grated parmesan cheese, divided	120 ml
1 (12 ounce) package shredded mozzarella cheese, divided	340 g

- Brown ground beef and onion in large skillet. Add garlic powder, spaghetti sauce and oregano. Cook just until thoroughly warm.

- Spoon layer of meat sauce in sprayed, oval slow cooker. Add layer of uncooked lasagna noodles (break to fit slow cooker).

- Top with layer of half remaining meat sauce, half cottage cheese, half parmesan cheese and half mozzarella cheese. Repeat layers and start with more lasagna noodles.

- Cover and cook on LOW for 6 to 8 hours. Serves 4 to 6.

Mac 'N Cheese Supper

1½ pounds lean ground beef	.7 kg
2 (7 ounce) packages macaroni and cheese dinners	2 (198 g)
1 (15 ounce) can whole kernel corn, drained	425 g
1½ cups shredded Monterey Jack cheese	360 ml

- In large skillet, sprinkle ground beef with 1 teaspoon (5 ml) salt, brown until no longer pink and drain.

- Prepare macaroni and cheese according to package directions.

- Spray 5-quart (5 L) slow cooker.   Spoon in beef, macaroni and corn and mix well.

- Cover and cook on LOW for 4 to 5 hours.

- When ready to serve, sprinkle Jack cheese over top and leave in cooker until cheese melts.
  Serves 4 to 6.

Meat on the Table

1½ - 2 pounds lean ground beef	**.7 kg**
1 (1 ounce) packet beefy onion soup mix	**28 g**
⅓ cup quick oats	**160 ml**
2 eggs	
1 (12 ounce) bottle chili sauce, divided	**340 g**

- Make foil handles for slow cooker. (See page 192). Spray 5 to 6-quart (5 L) oval slow cooker.

- In bowl, combine beef, onion soup mix, oats, eggs, ¾ cup (180 ml) chili sauce and 1 teaspoon (5 ml) black pepper and mix well.

- With your hands, shape meat mixture into round ball, place in slow cooker and pat down into loaf shape.

- Cover and cook on LOW for 3 to 4 hours.

- Before last half hour of cooking time, spread remaining chili sauce over top of loaf and continue cooking.

- Use foil handles to lift meat loaf out of slow cooker. Serves 4 to 6.

Jack's Meat Loaf

2 pounds lean ground beef	**1 kg**
2 eggs	
½ cup chili sauce	**120 ml**
1¼ cups dry, seasoned breadcrumbs	**300 ml**
1 (8 ounce) package shredded Monterey Jack	
cheese, divided	**227 g**

- Make foil handles for slow cooker. (See page 192).

- Combine beef, eggs, chili sauce and breadcrumbs in bowl and mix well.

- With your hands, shape half beef mixture into flat loaf and place in sprayed slow cooker.

- Sprinkle half cheese over meat loaf and press into meat.

- Form remaining meat mixture in same shape as first layer, place over cheese and seal seams.

- Cover and cook on LOW for 6 to 7 hours.

- When ready to serve, sprinkle remaining cheese over loaf and leave in cooker until cheese melts.

- Carefully remove loaf with foil handles and place on serving plate. Serves 4 to 6.

Hashbrown Dinner

1½ pounds lean ground chuck, browned	.7 kg
1 (1 ounce) packet dry brown gravy mix	28 g
1 (15 ounce) can cream-style corn	425 g
1 (15 ounce) can whole kernel corn	425 g
1 (8 ounce) package shredded cheddar cheese, divided	227 g
1 (16 ounce) package frozen hashbrowns, partially thawed	.5 kg
1 (10 ounce) can golden mushroom soup	280 g
1 (5 ounce) can evaporated milk	143 g

- Place browned beef in sprayed slow cooker and toss with dry brown gravy.

- Add cream corn and whole kernel corn and cover with half cheddar cheese.

- Top with hashbrowns and remaining cheese.

- In bowl, combine mushroom soup and evaporated milk. Mix well and pour over hashbrowns and cheese. Cover and cook on LOW for 6 to 8 hours. Serves 4 to 6.

Fiesta Beef and Rice

1½ pounds lean ground beef	**.7 kg**
1 (15 ounce) can Mexican stewed tomatoes	**425 g**
1 (7 ounce) box beef-flavored rice mix	**198 g**
1 (11 ounce) can Mexicorn®, drained	**312 g**
Salsa	

- Sprinkle salt and pepper over ground beef and shape into small patties.

- Place in sprayed 5-quart (5 L) oval slow cooker.

- In separate bowl, combine stewed tomatoes, rice, corn and 2 cups (480 ml) water and mix well. Spoon over beef patties.

- Cover and cook on LOW for 4 to 5 hours.

- When ready to serve, place large spoonful of salsa on each serving. Serves 4 to 6.

Cowboy Feed

1½ pounds lean ground beef	.7 kg
2 onions, coarsely chopped	
5 medium potatoes, peeled, sliced	
1 (15 ounce) can kidney beans, rinsed, drained	425 g
1 (15 ounce) can pinto beans, drained	425 g
1 (15 ounce) can Mexican stewed tomatoes	425 g
1 (10 ounce) can tomato soup	280 g
½ teaspoon basil	2 ml
½ teaspoon oregano	2 ml
2 teaspoons minced garlic	10 ml

- In skillet, sprinkle beef with some salt and pepper, brown and drain.

- Place onions in slow cooker and spoon beef over onions.

- On top of beef, layer potatoes and kidney and pinto beans.

- Pour stewed tomatoes and tomato soup over beans and potatoes and sprinkle with basil, oregano and garlic.

- Cover and cook on LOW for 7 to 8 hours. Serves 4 to 6.

Cheeseburger Supper

1 (5 ounce) box bacon and cheddar scalloped potatoes	143 g
⅓ cup milk	80 ml
¼ cup (½ stick) butter, melted	60 ml
1 (15 ounce) can whole kernel corn with liquid	425 g
1½ pounds lean ground beef	.7 kg
1 onion, coarsely chopped	
1 (8 ounce) package shredded cheddar cheese	227 g

- Place scalloped potatoes in sprayed slow cooker.

- Pour 2¼ cups (540 ml) boiling water, milk and butter over potatoes.

- In skillet, brown ground beef and onion in little oil, drain and spoon over potatoes. Top with corn.

- Cover and cook on LOW for 6 to 7 hours.

- When ready to serve, sprinkle cheese over corn. Serves 4 to 6.

Beef and Macaroni Supper

1 (10 ounce) package macaroni, cooked, drained	280 g
3 tablespoons oil	45 ml
1½ pounds lean ground beef, browned, drained	.7 kg
1 onion, chopped	
3 ribs celery, chopped	
2 (10 ounce) cans tomato soup	2 (280 g)
1 (6 ounce) can tomato paste	168 g
1 teaspoon beef bouillon granules	5 ml
1 (8 ounce) package cubed Velveeta® cheese	227 g

- Toss cooked macaroni with oil to make sure macaroni does not stick.

- Place in sprayed slow cooker.

- Add beef, onion, celery, tomato soup, tomato paste, beef bouillon and ⅓ cup (160 m) water and stir to mix well.

- Cover and cook on LOW for 4 to 6 hours. Before last hour of cooking time, stir in cubed cheese. Serves 4 to 6.

Beef-Bean Medley

1 pound lean ground beef	.5 kg
1 onion, chopped	
6 slices bacon, cooked, crumbled	
2 (15 ounce) cans pork and beans	2 (425 g)
1 (15 ounce) can butter beans, rinsed, drained	425 g
1 (15 ounce) can kidney beans, rinsed, drained	425 g
½ cup packed brown sugar	120 ml
3 tablespoons vinegar	45 ml
1 (13 ounce) bag original corn chips	370 g
1 (8 ounce) package shredded cheddar cheese	227 g

- In skillet, brown ground beef, drain and transfer to sprayed 4 to 5-quart (4 L) slow cooker.

- Add bacon and all 3 cans of beans.

- In bowl, combine ketchup, brown sugar and vinegar. Add to cooker and stir.

- Cover and cook on LOW for 4 to 6 hours.

- When ready to serve, spoon over corn chips and sprinkle cheese over top. Serves 4 to 6.

Italian Tortellini

½ pound ground round steak	227 g
1 (1 pound) package bulk Italian sausage	.5 kg
1 (15 ounce) carton refrigerated marinara sauce	425 g
1 (15 ounce) can Italian stewed tomatoes with liquid	425 g
1½ cups sliced fresh mushrooms	360 ml
1 (9 ounce) package refrigerated cheese tortellini	255g
1½ cups shredded mozzarella cheese	360 ml

- Brown and cook ground beef and sausage in large skillet about 10 minutes on medium-low heat and drain.

- In 4 to 5-quart (4 L) slow cooker, combine meat mixture, marinara sauce, tomatoes and mushrooms.

- Cover and cook on LOW 6 to 8 hours.

- Stir in tortellini and sprinkle with mozzarella cheese.

- Turn cooker to HIGH and continue cooking for additional 10 to 15 minutes or until tortellini is tender. Serves 4 to 6.

Sloppy Joes

3 pounds ground beef	1.3 kg
1 tablespoon minced garlic	15 ml
1 large onion, finely chopped	
2 ribs celery, chopped	
¼ cup packed brown sugar	60 ml
3½ tablespoons mustard	50 ml
1 tablespoon chili powder	15 ml
1½ cups ketchup	360 ml
3 tablespoons Worcestershire sauce	45 ml

- Brown beef, garlic and onion in very large skillet and drain.

- Combine celery, brown sugar, mustard, chili powder, ketchup and Worcestershire in sprayed 5-quart (5 L) slow cooker. Stir in meat mixture.

- Cover and cook on LOW heat for 6 to 7 hours. Serves 6 to 8.

TIP: This will make enough to fill 16 to 18 hamburger buns.

Special Hot Dog Supper

1 pound beef wieners	**.5 kg**
2 (15 ounce) cans chili without beans	**2 (425 g)**
1 onion, finely chopped	
1 (10 ounce) can cheddar cheese soup	**280 g**
1 (10 ounce) can fiesta nacho cheese soup	**280 g**
1 (7 ounce) can chopped green chilies, drained	**198 g**

- Cut wieners in ½-inch (1.2 cm) pieces and place in sprayed slow cooker.

- In saucepan, combine chili, onion, cheese soup, nacho cheese soup and green chilies.
  (Omit green chilies if serving to kids.)

- Heat just enough to mix ingredients well.
  Spoon over wieners.

- Cover and cook on LOW for 1 hour 30 minutes to 2 hours.

- Serve over bowl of small corn chips or crisp tortilla chips slightly crushed. Serves 4 to 6.

PORK

Stuffed Pork Chops

4 - 5 (1 inch) thick pork chops	**4 - 5 (2.5 cm)**
1 (15 ounce) can mixed vegetables, well drained	**425 g**
1 (8 ounce) can whole kernel corn, drained	**227 g**
½ cup rice	**120 ml**
1 cup Italian-seasoned breadcrumbs	**240 ml**
1 (15 ounce) can stewed tomatoes, slightly drained	**425 g**

- Cut pocket in each pork chop and season with a little salt and pepper.

- In large bowl combine vegetables, corn, rice and breadcrumbs and stuff pork chops with vegetable mixture. Secure open sides with toothpicks.

- Place remaining vegetable mixture in bottom of 5-quart (5 L) slow cooker. Add pork chops and spoon stewed tomatoes over top of pork chops.

- Cover and cook on LOW for 8 to 9 hours.

- Serve vegetable mixture along with pork chops. Serves 4 to 5.

Smothered Pork Chop Dinner

6 (¾ inch) thick bone-in pork chops	6 (1.8 cm)
8 - 10 medium red (new) potatoes with peels	
2 onions, sliced	
1 (10 ounce) can cream of chicken soup	280 g
¼ cup dijon-style mustard	60 ml
1 teaspoon dried basil leaves	5 ml

- In non-stick skillet, brown pork chops sprinkled with a little salt and pepper. Place potatoes and onions in 5 or 6-quart (5 L) slow cooker and add browned pork chops.

- In saucepan, combine soup, broth, mustard and basil leaves. Heat just enough to mix well and pour over pork chops. Cover and cook on LOW for 7 to 9 hours. Serves 4 to 6.

TIP: To "dress" the pork chops, add 1 (3 ounce/84 g) can fried onion rings.

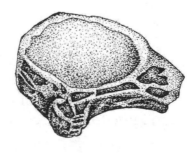

Savory Pork Chops

6 (¾ inch) thick pork chops	6 (1.8 cm)
1 cup pineapple juice	240 ml
⅓ cup packed brown sugar	80 ml
3 tablespoons cider vinegar	45 ml

- In skillet, brown pork chops on both sides and place in 5-quart (5 L) slow cooker.

- Combine pineapple juice, brown sugar and vinegar and mix well.

- Pour brown sugar-vinegar mixture over pork chops.

- Cover and cook on LOW for 4 to 5 hours.

- Serve over hot, cooked noodles. Serves 4 to 6.

Ranch Pork Chops

6 (¾ inch) thick bone-in pork chops	6 (1.8 cm)
1 (1 ounce) packet ranch dressing mix	28 g
2 (15 ounce) cans new potatoes, drained, quartered	2 (425 g)
1 (10 ounce) can French onion soup	280 g

- Place pork chops on bottom of sprayed 6-quart (6 L) oval slow cooker.

- Sprinkle pork chops with ranch dressing mix and ½ teaspoon (2 ml) pepper.

- Place potatoes around pork chops and pour French onion soup around potatoes and chops.

- Cover and cook on LOW for 4 to 5 hours. Serves 4 to 6.

Pork Chops with Orange Sauce

2 medium sliced yellow squash	
2 onions, sliced	
6 - 8 bone-in pork chops	
½ cup chicken broth	**120 ml**
½ cup orange marmalade	**120 ml**
1 tablespoon honey-mustard	**15 ml**
2 tablespoons cornstarch	**30 ml**

- Place squash and onions in 5 to 6-quart (5 L) slow cooker.

- Sprinkle a little salt and pepper on top of pork chops and place over vegetables.

- In bowl combine broth, marmalade and mustard and spoon over pork chops.

- Cover and cook on LOW for 4 to 6 hours.

- Transfer pork chops and vegetables to serving plate and cover to keep warm.

- For sauce, pour liquid from slow cooker into medium saucepan. Combine 2 tablespoons (30 ml) water with cornstarch and add to saucepan.

- Heat mixture, stir constantly until thick and serve over pork chops and vegetables. Serves 6 to 8.

Pork Chops for Supper

6 (¾ inch) thick pork loin chops	6 (1.8 cm)
1 onion, halved, sliced	
1 (8 ounce) can tomato sauce	227 g
¼ cup packed brown sugar	60 ml
1 tablespoon Worcestershire sauce	15 ml
1 teaspoon seasoned salt	5 ml

- In skillet, brown pork chops on both sides and place in 4 to 5-quart (4 L) slow cooker. Place onions over pork chops.

- Combine tomato sauce, brown sugar, Worcestershire sauce, seasoned salt and ¼ cup (60 ml) water and spoon over onions and pork chops.

- Cover and cook on LOW for 4 to 5 hours. Serves 4 to 6.

Pork Chops and Gravy

6 (½ inch) thick pork chops	6 (1.2 cm)
8 - 10 new potatoes with peels, quartered	
1 (16 ounce) package baby carrots	.5 kg
2 (10 ounce) cans cream of mushroom soup	
with roasted garlic	2 (280 g)

- Sprinkle a little salt and pepper on pork chops.

- In skillet, brown pork chops and place in 5 to 6-quart (5 L) slow cooker. Place potatoes and carrots around pork chops.

- In saucepan, heat mushroom soup with ½ cup (120 ml) water and pour over chops and vegetables.

- Cover and cook on LOW for 6 to 7 hours. Serves 4 to 6.

Pork Chops Pizza

6 (1 inch) thick boneless pork chops	6 (2.5 cm)
Oil	
1 onion, finely chopped	
1 green bell pepper, finely chopped	
1 (8 ounce) jar pizza sauce	227 g
1 (10 ounce) box plain couscous	280 g
2 tablespoons butter	60 ml
1 cup shredded mozzarella cheese	240 ml

- Trim fat from pork chops and sprinkle with a little salt and pepper. In skillet, brown and cook pork chops on both sides for 5 minutes. Transfer chops to sprayed, oval slow cooker. Spoon onion and bell pepper over chops and pour pizza sauce over top.

- Cover and cook on LOW for 4 to 6 hours. Cook couscous according to package directions except add 2 tablespoons (30 ml) butter instead of 1 tablespoon (15 ml) and place on serving platter. Spoon chops and sauce over couscous and sprinkle cheese over chops. Serves 4 to 6.

Pineapple-Pork Chops

6 - 8 (½ inch) thick boneless pork chops	6 - 8 (1.2 cm)
1 (6 ounce) can frozen pineapple juice concentrate, thawed	168 g
¼ cup packed brown sugar	60 ml
⅓ cup wine or tarragon vinegar	80 ml
⅓ cup honey	80 ml
1 (6 ounce) package parmesan-butter rice	168 g

- In skillet, brown pork chops in a little oil and transfer to sprayed slow cooker.

- In bowl, combine pineapple juice, sugar, vinegar and honey. Pour over pork chops.

- Cover and cook on LOW for 5 to 6 hours. Serve over hot, buttered rice. Serves 6 to 8.

Delicious Pork Chops

1¾ cups flour	420 ml
Scant 2 tablespoons dry mustard	30 ml
8 boneless, thick pork chops	
Oil	
1 (10 ounce) can chicken and rice soup	280 g

- Place flour and mustard in shallow bowl. Dredge pork chops in flour-mustard mixture.

- In skillet, brown pork chops in a little oil. Place all chops in 6-quart (6 L) oval slow cooker.

- Pour soup over pork and add about ¼ cup (60 ml) water. Cover and cook on LOW for 6 to 8 hours. Serves 6 to 8.

Peachy Pork Chops

6 - 8 (¾ inch) thick bone-in pork chops	**6 - 8 (1.8cm)**
½ cup packed brown sugar	**120 ml**
¼ teaspoon ground cinnamon	**1 ml**
¼ teaspoon ground cloves	**1 ml**
1 (8 ounce) can tomato sauce	**227 g**
1 (28 ounce) can peach halves with juice	**794 g**
¼ cup white vinegar	**60 ml**

- In skillet, brown pork chops on both sides and place in oval slow cooker. Combine sugar, cinnamon, cloves, tomato sauce, ¼ cup (60 ml) syrup from peaches and vinegar.

- Pour sugar-tomato sauce mixture over pork chops and place peach halves over top. Cover and cook on LOW for 4 to 5 hours. Serves 6 to 8.

Italian Pork Chops

6 - 8 (1 inch) thick boneless pork chops	6 - 8 (2.5 cm)
½ pound fresh mushrooms, sliced	227 g
1 (10 ounce) package frozen onion-bell pepper blend, thawed	280 g
1 teaspoon Italian seasoning	5 ml
1 (15 ounce) can Italian stewed tomatoes	425 g

- In skillet, brown pork chops and sprinkle with salt and pepper on both sides. In 6-quart (6 L) slow cooker, combine mushrooms, onion-bell pepper blend and Italian seasoning and set aside.

- Place pork chops over vegetables and pour stewed tomatoes over pork chops. Cover and cook on LOW for 7 to 8 hours. To serve, spoon mushroom-seasoning blend over pork chops. Serves 6 to 8.

Honey-Mustard Pork Chops

Try this sauce over hot, cooked rice. It is wonderful!

1 (10 ounce) can golden mushroom soup	280 g
⅓ cup white wine	80 ml
¼ cup honey-mustard	60 ml
1 teaspoon minced garlic	5 ml
4 - 5 (¾ inch) thick pork chops	4 - 5
	(1.8 cm)

- In large bowl, combine soup, wine, honey-mustard, minced garlic and 1 teaspoon (5 ml) salt and mix well.

- Place pork chops, sprinkled with a little black pepper, in 5-quart (5 L) slow cooker and spoon soup honey-mustard mixture over chops.

- Cover and cook on LOW for 5 to 6 hours.

- When ready to serve, lift pork chops out of sauce and onto serving plate. Stir sauce to mix well and serve with chops. Serves 4 to 5.

Tip: For a "meat and potato meal", just slice 3 potatoes and place in slow cooker before adding pork chops.

"Baked" Pork Chops

6 - 8 (½ inch) thick pork chops	6 - 8 (1.2 cm)
1 (10 ounce) can cream of chicken soup	280 g
3 tablespoons ketchup	45 ml
1 tablespoon Worcestershire sauce	15 ml
1 onion, chopped	

- In skillet, brown pork chops in a little oil and season with a little salt and pepper. Place pork chops in sprayed slow cooker. In bowl, combine chicken soup, ketchup, Worcestershire and onion and pour over pork chops. Cover and cook on LOW for 5 to 6 hours. Serves 6 to 8.

Tender Pork Loin

1 (3 - 4 pound) pork loin	1.3 kg
2 teaspoons minced garlic	10 ml
½ teaspoon rosemary	2 ml
1 teaspoon sage	5 ml
1½ teaspoons marjoram	7 ml

- Place pork loin in slow cooker, rub with minced garlic and sprinkle with rosemary, sage and marjoram. Add about ¼ cup (60 ml) water to slow cooker. Cover and cook on LOW heat for 4 to 5 hours. Serves 6 to 8.

TIP: Sometimes it is hard to buy a small (3 to 4 pound/1.3 kg) pork loin, but they are available in (8 or 9 pound/3.6 kg) sizes. Because pork loin is such a good cut of pork (no bones – no fat), you can buy a whole loin, cut it into 2 or 3 pieces and freeze the pieces not used.

Pork Roast with Apricot Glaze

1 (3 pound) boneless pork roast	1.3 kg
⅓ cup chicken broth	80 ml
1 (18 ounce) jar apricot preserves	510 g
2 tablespoons dijon-style mustard	30 ml
1 onion, finely chopped	
1 green bell pepper, finely chopped	

- Trim fat from roast and, if necessary, cut roast to fit into sprayed 4 to 5-quart (4 L) slow cooker. Place in roast in cooker.

- In saucepan combine broth, preserves, mustard, onion and bell pepper and heat just enough to mix ingredients well and pour over roast.

- Cover and cook on LOW for 9 to 10 hours or on HIGH for 5 to 6 hours.

- Transfer meat to serving plate.

- Sauce left in cooker is delicious as is or thicker. To thicken sauce, mix 1 tablespoon (15 ml) cornstarch and 2 tablespoons (30 ml) water. Place in saucepan and add sauce from cooker.

- Heat sauce and stir constantly until sauce thickens slightly.

- Sauce may be served with hot, cooked rice or just spoon over roast. Serves 6 to 8.

Fruit-Stuffed Pork Roast

1 (3 - 3½ pound) boneless pork loin roast	1.3 kg
1 cup mixed dried fruits	240 ml
1 tablespoon dried onion flakes	15 ml
1 teaspoon thyme leaves	5 ml
½ teaspoon ground cinnamon	2 ml
2 tablespoons oil	30 ml
½ cup apple cider	120 ml

- Place pork on cutting board. Cut horizontally through center of pork almost to opposite side. Open pork like a book.

- Layer dried fruits and onion in opening. Bring halves of pork together and tie at 1-inch intervals with kitchen twine.

- In small bowl, combine 1 teaspoon (5 ml) salt, thyme, cinnamon and ½ teaspoon (2 ml) black pepper and rub into roast.

- Place roast in skillet with oil and brown roast on all sides.

- Place roast in sprayed slow cooker and pour apple cider in bottom of cooker.

- Cover and cook on LOW for 3 to 4 hours. Partially cool before slicing. Serves 6 to 8.

Country Pork Chops

7 - 8 new potatoes with peels, sliced	
2 onions, sliced	
1 (10 ounce) can cream of celery soup	280 g
⅓ cup chicken broth	80 ml
3 tablespoons dijon-style mustard	45 ml
1 (4 ounce) can sliced mushrooms, drained	114 g
1 teaspoon minced garlic	5 ml
¾ teaspoon dried basil	4 ml
8 boneless pork chops	

- Place potatoes and onions in large slow cooker.

- In bowl, combine soup, broth, mustard, mushrooms, garlic and basil, mix well and pour over potatoes and onions. Stir to coat vegetables.

- Sprinkle pork chops with a little salt and pepper. In skillet brown both sides of pork chops in a little oil.

- Place chops over vegetables.

- Cover and cook on LOW for 6 to 7 hours. Serves 6 to 8.

Spinach-Stuffed Pork Roast

1 (2 - 2½ pound) pork tenderloin	1 kg
1 (10 ounce) package frozen chopped spinach, thawed	280 g
⅓ cup seasoned breadcrumbs	80 ml
⅓ cup grated parmesan cheese	80 ml
2 tablespoons oil	30 ml
½ teaspoon seasoned salt	2 ml

- Cut tenderloin horizontally lengthwise about ½-inch (1.2 cm) from top to within ¾-inch (1.8 cm) of opposite end and open flat.

- Turn pork to cut other side, from inside edge to outer edge, and open flat. If one side is thicker than other side, cover with plastic wrap and pound until both sides are ¾-inch (1.8 cm) thick.

- Squeeze spinach with several sheets of paper towels several times until all liquid is gone.

- Combine spinach, garlic, breadcrumbs and cheese and mix well.

- Spread mixture on inside surfaces of pork and press down. Roll pork and tie with kitchen twine.

- Heat oil in large skillet over medium-high heat and brown pork on all sides.

- Place in oval slow cooker and sprinkle with salt. Cover and cook on LOW for 6 to 8 hours. Serves 4 to 6.

Pork and Cabbage Supper

1 (16 ounce) package baby carrots	.5 kg
1 (1 ounce) packet golden onion soup mix	28 g
1 cup chicken broth	240 ml
1 (3 - 4 pound) pork shoulder roast	1.3 kg
1 medium head cabbage	

- Place carrots in 5-quart (5 L) slow cooker.

- Add chicken broth and 1 cup (240 ml) water. Sprinkle dry soup mix and lots of black pepper over carrots.

- Cut roast in half (if needed to fit in cooker) and place over carrot mixture. Cover and cook on LOW for 6 to 7 hours.

- Cut cabbage in small-size chunks and place over roast. Cover and cook additional 1 to 2 hours or until cabbage cooks. Serves 6 to 8.

Home-Style Ribs

4 - 6 pounds boneless pork spareribs	1.8 kg
1 cup chili sauce	240 ml
1 cup packed brown sugar	240 ml
2 tablespoons vinegar	30 ml
2 tablespoons Worcestershire sauce	30 ml

- Sprinkle ribs liberally with salt and pepper. Place ribs in slow cooker.

- Combine ½ cup (120 ml) water, chili sauce, brown sugar, vinegar and Worcestershire and spoon over ribs.

- Cover and cook on LOW for 5 to 6 hours. Serves 6 to 8.

Roasted Red Pepper Tenderloin

2 pounds pork tenderloin	1 kg
1 (1 ounce) packet ranch dressing mix	28 g
1 cup roasted red bell peppers, rinsed, chopped	240 ml
1 (8 ounce) carton sour cream	227 g

- In large skillet, brown tenderloins and place in 6-quart (6 L) oval slow cooker.

- Combine ranch dressing mix, red bell peppers and ½ cup (120 ml) water and spoon over tenderloins.

- Cover and cook on LOW for 4 to 5 hours.

- When ready to serve, remove tenderloins from slow cooker.

- Stir sour cream into sauce. Serve over tenderloin slices. Serves 4 to 6.

Walnut Ham

½ pound cooked, ham slices	227 g
2 (10 ounce) cans cream of onion soup	2 (280 g)
⅓ cup grated parmesan cheese	80 ml
⅓ cup chopped walnuts	160 ml
Hot cooked linguine	

- Cut ham into ½-inch (1.2 cm) strips.

- Place soups, cheese, walnuts and ham strips in slow cooker.

- Cover and cook on LOW for 1 to 2 hours or until hot and bubbly.

- Serve over hot, cooked linguine. Serves 4.

Honey-Mustard Pork Roast

1 green bell pepper, chopped	
1 sweet red bell pepper, chopped	
2 yellow onions, chopped	
3 tablespoons sweet and tangy honey-mustard	45 ml
1 (2 - 2 ½ pound) pork loin roast	1 kg

- Combine bell peppers and onions in 4 to 6-quart (4 L) slow cooker. Rub honey-mustard liberally over pork loin with most of honey-mustard on top.

- Cook on LOW for 4 to 6 hours and place in serving platter. Spoon bell peppers, onions and pan juices in small serving bowl and spoon over slices of roast to serve. Serves 4 to 6.

Delectable Apricot Ribs

4 - 5 pounds baby back pork ribs	1.8 kg
1 (16 ounce) jar apricot preserves	.5 kg
⅓ cup soy sauce	80 ml
¼ cup packed light brown sugar	60 ml
2 teaspoons garlic powder	10 ml

- Spray large slow cooker and place ribs in cooker.

- In bowl, combine preserves, soy sauce, brown sugar and garlic powder and spoon over ribs.

- Cover and cook on LOW for 6 to 7 hours. Serves 8 to 10.

Ginger Pork

1 (2 - 2 ½ pound) boneless pork roast	1 kg
1 cup chicken broth	240 ml
3½ tablespoons quick-cooking tapioca	50 ml
3 tablespoons soy sauce	45 ml
1 teaspoon grated fresh ginger	5 ml
1 (15 ounce) can pineapple chunks with juice	425 g
1 (16 ounce) package baby carrots	.5 kg
1 (8 ounce) can sliced water chestnuts, drained	227 g

- Trim fat from pork. Cut pork into 1-inch (2.5 cm) pieces, brown in large skillet and drain.

- In sprayed 4 to 5-quart (5 L) slow cooker combine chicken broth, tapioca, soy sauce, ginger, pineapple juice, carrots and water chestnuts. (Chill pineapple chunks in refrigerator until ready to include in recipe.)

- Add browned pork. Cover and cook on LOW for 6 to 8 hours.

- Turn heat to HIGH and stir in pineapple chunks. Cover and cook for additional 10 minutes.

- Serve over hot, cooked rice. Serves 4 to 6.

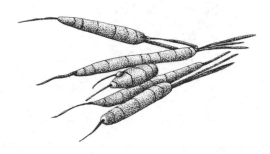

Barbecue Pork Roast

Use leftovers for great sandwiches.

1 onion, thinly sliced	
2 tablespoons flour	30 ml
1 (2 - 3 pound) pork shoulder roast	1 kg
1 (8 ounce) bottle barbecue sauce	227 g
1 tablespoon chili powder	15 ml
1 teaspoon ground cumin	5 ml

- Separate onion slices into rings and place in 4 to 5-quart (4 L) slow cooker. Sprinkle flour over onions. If necessary, cut roast to fit cooker and place over onions. In bowl, combine barbecue sauce, chili powder and cumin and pour over roast.

- Cover and cook on LOW for 8 to 10 hours. Remove roast from cooker and slice. Serve sauce over sliced roast. Serves 6 to 8.

Tip: To make sandwiches, shred roast and return to cooker. Cook additional 30 minutes to heat thoroughly.

Tangy Apricot Ribs

3 - 4 pounds baby back pork ribs	1.3 kg
1 (16 ounce) jar apricot preserves	.5 kg
1/3 cup soy sauce	80 ml
1/4 cup packed light brown sugar	60 ml

- Place ribs in large, sprayed slow cooker.

- In bowl combine preserves, soy sauce and brown sugar and spoon over ribs.

- Cover and cook on LOW for 6 to 8 hours. Serves 6 to 8.

Finger Lickin' Baby Backs

2½ - 3 pounds baby back pork ribs	1.2 kg
½ cup chili sauce	120 ml
1/3 cup apple cider vinegar	80 ml
½ cup packed brown sugar	120 ml

- Spray sides of 5 to 6-quart (5 L) slow cooker. Cut ribs in serving-size pieces, sprinkle with black pepper and place in slow cooker. Combine chili sauce, vinegar, brown sugar and about ¾ cup (180 ml) water and pour over ribs.

- Cover and cook on LOW for about 6 to 7 hours. After about 3 hours, you might move ribs around in slow cooker so sauce is spread over all ribs. Serves 4 to 6.

Zesty Ham Supper

1 (28 ounce) package frozen hashbrown potatoes with onions and peppers, thawed	794 g
3 cups cooked, diced ham	710 ml
1 (10 ounce) box frozen green peas, thawed	280 g
2 (10 ounce) cans fiesta nacho cheese soup	2 (280 g)
1 cup milk	240 ml
1 bunch fresh green onions, chopped	

- Place potatoes, ham and peas in sprayed 6-quart (6 L) slow cooker and stir to mix.

- In bowl, combine soup and milk and mix well. Pour over potato mixture and mix well.

- Cover and cook on LOW for 6 to 8 hours.

- Sprinkle green onions over top when ready to serve. Serves 6 to 8.

Apricot Ham

1 (6 - 8 pound) butt or shank ham	2.7 kg
Whole cloves	
2 tablespoons dry mustard	30 ml
1¼ cups apricot jam	300 ml
1¼ cups packed light brown sugar	300 ml

- Place ham, fat-side up, in slow cooker. Stick lots of whole cloves on outside of ham.

- In bowl, combine mustard, jam and brown sugar and spread all over ham. Cover and cook on LOW for 5 to 6 hours. Serves 8 to 10.

Saucy Ham Loaf

Great with sweet and hot mustard recipe below

1 pound ground ham	.5 kg
8 ounces ground beef	227 g
8 ounces ground pork	227 g
2 eggs, slightly beaten	
1 cup Italian-seasoned breadcrumbs	240 ml
1 (5 ounce) can evaporated milk	143 g
¼ cup chili sauce	60 ml
1 teaspoon seasoned salt	5 ml

- Combine all ingredients and form into loaf in sprayed, oval slow cooker. Shape loaf so that neither end touches sides of cooker.

- Cover and cook on LOW for 6 to 7 hours. Serve with Sweet-and-Hot Mustard. Serves 4 to 6.

Sweet-and-Hot Mustard:

Use on Ham Loaf or ham sandwiches.

4 ounces dry mustard	114 g
1 cup vinegar	240 ml
3 eggs, beaten	
1 cup sugar	240 ml

- Mix mustard and vinegar until smooth and let stand overnight.

- Add eggs and sugar and cook in double boiler 8 to 10 minutes or until it coats the spoon. Cool and store in covered jars in refrigerator. Serve with Saucy Ham Loaf.

Ham Loaf
Great for leftover ham

1½ pounds cooked, ground ham	.7 kg
1 pound ground turkey	.5 kg
2 eggs	
1 cup seasoned breadcrumbs	240 ml
2 teaspoons chicken seasoning	10 ml

- In bowl, combine ground ham, ground turkey, eggs, seasoned breadcrumbs and 2 teaspoons (10 ml) chicken seasoning and mix well.

- Use hands to pick up loaf mixture and shape into short loaf that will fit into oval slow cooker.

- Cover and cook on LOW for 4 to 5 hours.

- Serve with Cherry Sauce. Serves 4 to 6.

Cherry Sauce:

1 cup cherry preserves	240 ml
2 tablespoons cider vinegar	30 ml
Scant ⅛ teaspoon ground cloves	.5 ml
Scant ⅛ teaspoon ground cinnamon	.5 ml

- Place cherry preserves, vinegar and spices in saucepan and heat. Serve over slices of Ham Loaf.

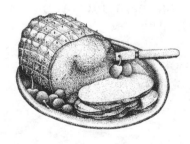

Ham and Potato Dish

4 large baking potatoes	
3 cups cubed leftover ham	710 ml
1 (10 ounce) box frozen whole kernel corn, drained	280 g
1 (10 ounce) package frozen onion-pepper blend, thawed	280 g
1 teaspoon seasoned salt	5 ml
2 (10 ounce) cans fiesta nacho cheese soup	2 (280 g)
½ cup milk	120 ml
1 (3 ounce) can fried onion rings	84 g

- Cut potatoes into 1-inch (2.5 cm) cubes.

- In slow cooker combine potatoes, ham, corn, onions and peppers and seasoned salt. Heat cheese soup and milk just enough to mix well. Add to slow cooker and mix with ingredients.

- Cover and cook on LOW for 5 to 6 hours or until potatoes are tender. When ready to serve, sprinkle onions over top. Serves 4 to 6.

Ben's Ham and Rice

1 (6.7 ounce) box brown-wild rice, mushroom recipe	170 g
3 - 4 cups cooked, chopped or cubed ham	710 ml
1 (4 ounce) can sliced mushrooms, drained	114 g
1 (10 ounce) package frozen green peas	280 g
2 cups chopped celery	480 ml

- In 4 to 5-quart (4 L) slow cooker, combine rice, seasoning packet, ham, mushrooms, peas, celery plus 2⅓ cups (640 ml) water. Stir to mix well.

- Cover and cook on LOW for 2 to 4 hours. Serves 4 to 6.

Creamy Potatoes and Ham

5 medium potatoes, peeled, sliced, divided	
1 onion, chopped, divided	
2 cups cooked, cubed ham, divided	480 ml
1 (8 ounce) package cubed Velveeta® cheese, divided	227 g
1 (10 ounce) can broccoli-cheese soup	280 g
¼ cup milk	60 ml

- In slow cooker, layer half each of potatoes, 1 teaspoon (5 ml) salt, onion, ham and cheese and repeat layer. In bowl, combine soup and milk until fairly smooth.

- Cover and cook on HIGH for 1 hour. Reduce heat to LOW and cook for 6 to 7 hours. Serves 4.

Creamed Ham with Spaghetti

2 (10 ounce) cans cream of mushroom soup with roasted garlic	2 (280 g)
1 cup sliced fresh mushrooms	240 ml
2 - 2½ cups cooked, cubed ham	480 ml
1 (5 ounce) can evaporated milk	143 g
1 (7 ounce) box ready-cut spaghetti	198 g

- In slow cooker, combine soups, mushrooms, ham, evaporated milk and a little salt and pepper.

- Cover, cook on LOW for 2 hours and mix well.

- In saucepan, cook spaghetti and drain. Add spaghetti to slow cooker and toss to coat.
  Serves 4 to 6.

Ham to the Rescue

2½ cups ground, cooked ham	600 ml
⅓ cup crushed white cheddar Cheez-Its® crackers	160 ml
1 large egg	
⅓ cup chili sauce	80 ml
4 medium potatoes, peeled, sliced	
1 green bell pepper, cored, seeded, julienned	
1 (8 ounce) package shredded cheddar-Jack cheese	227 g
1 (5 ounce) can evaporated milk	143 g
1 teaspoon seasoned salt	5 ml

- In bowl, combine ham, crushed crackers, egg and chili sauce and mix well.

- With hands, shape ham mixture into 6 patties and set aside.

- In skillet, saute potatoes in a little oil and turn several times to brown lightly on both sides. Place potatoes and bell pepper in 6-quart (6 L) slow cooker.

- In another bowl, combine cheese, evaporated milk and seasoned salt and pour over potatoes.

- Place ham patties over potatoes.

- Cover and cook on LOW for 3 to 4 hours. Serves 4 to 6.

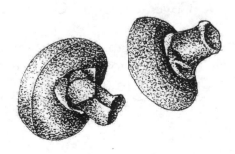

Sweet-and-Sour Sausage Links

2 (16 ounce) packages miniature smoked sausage links	2 (.5 kg)
¾ cup chili sauce	180 ml
1 cup packed brown sugar	240 ml
¼ cup horseradish	60 ml

- Place sausages in 4-quart (4 L) slow cooker.

- Combine chili sauce, brown sugar and horseradish and pour over sausages.

- Cover and cook on LOW for 4 hours. Serves 4 to 6.

TIP: This can be served as an appetizer or served over hot, cooked rice.

Tortellini Italian-Style

2 pounds bulk Italian sausage	1 kg
1 (15 ounce) carton refrigerated marinara sauce	425 g
2 cups sliced fresh mushrooms, sliced	480 ml
1 (15 ounce) cans Italian stewed tomatoes	425 g
1 (9 ounce) package refrigerated cheese tortellini	255 g
1½ cups shredded mozzarella cheese	360 ml

- In skillet, brown and cook sausage for 10 to 15 minutes and drain well. In sprayed 5-quart (5 L) slow cooker, combine sausage, marinara sauce, mushrooms and tomatoes.

- Cover and cook on LOW 6 to 7 hours. Stir in tortellini and sprinkle with cheese.

- Cover and cook on HIGH about 15 minutes or until tortellini is tender. Serves 4 to 6.

Sausage and Beans

1 (1 pound) fully cooked smoked, link sausage	.5 kg
2 (15 ounce) cans baked beans	2 (425 g)
1 (15 ounce) can great northern beans, drained	425 g
1 (15 ounce) can pinto beans, drained	425 g
½ cup chili sauce	120 ml
⅓ cup packed brown sugar	160 ml
1 tablespoon Worcestershire sauce	15 ml

- Cut link sausage into 1-inch (2.5 cm) slices. In slow cooker, layer sausage and beans.

- Combine chili sauce, brown sugar, a little black pepper and Worcestershire sauce and pour over beans and sausage.

- Cover and cook on LOW for 4 hours. Stir before serving. Serves 4.

Sauerkraut and Bratwurst

1 (28 ounce) jar refrigerated sauerkraut	794 g
¾ cup beer	180 ml
1 tablespoon white wine Worcestershire sauce	15 ml
1 (1 ounce) packet dry onion soup mix	28 g
2 pounds pre-cooked bratwurst	1 kg

- In 4 to 5-quart (4 L) slow cooker, combine sauerkraut, beer, Worcestershire and onion soup mix and mix well. Cut bratwurst in diagonal slices and place on top of sauerkraut-beer mixture.

- Cover and cook on LOW for 5 to 6 hours or on HIGH for 2 hours 30 minutes to 3 hours. Serves 4 to 6.

DESSERTS

Delicious Bread Pudding

8 cups cubed leftover hot rolls, cinnamon rolls or bread	2 L
2 cups milk	480 ml
4 large eggs	
¾ cup sugar	180 ml
⅓ cup packed brown sugar	80 ml
¼ cup (½ stick) butter, melted	60 ml
1 teaspoon vanilla extract	5 ml
¼ teaspoon nutmeg	1 ml
1 cup finely chopped pecans	240 ml

- Place cubed bread or rolls in sprayed slow cooker. In mixing bowl, combine, eggs, milk, vanilla, butter, both sugars and nutmeg and beat until smooth. Stir in pecans.

- Cover and cook on LOW for 3 hours. Serve with lemon sauce or whipped topping.

Baked Apples

4 - 5 large baking apples	
1 tablespoon lemon juice	**15 ml**
⅓ cup Craisins®	**80 ml**
½ cup chopped pecans	**120 ml**
¾ cup packed brown sugar	**180 ml**
½ teaspoon ground cinnamon	**2 ml**
¼ cup (½ stick) butter, softened	**60 ml**

- Scoop out center of each apple and leave cavity about ½ inch (1.2 cm) from bottom.

- Peel top of apples down about 1 inch (2.5 cm) and brush lemon juice on peeled edges.

- In bowl, combine Craisins®, pecans, brown sugar, cinnamon and butter. Spoon mixture into apple cavities.

- Pour ½ cup (120 ml) water in oval slow cooker and place apples on bottom.

- Cover and cook on LOW for 1 to 3 hours or until tender.

- Serve warm or room temperature drizzled with caramel ice cream topping.

Bread Pudding with Coconut and Nuts

1 cup sugar	240 ml
½ cup (1 stick) butter, softened	120 ml
1 teaspoon ground cinnamon	5 ml
4 eggs	
3 cups white bread cubes	710 ml
⅓ cup flaked coconut	80 ml
⅓ cup chopped pecans	80 ml

- In mixing bowl, beat sugar, butter and cinnamon. Add eggs and beat well until it blends. Stir in bread, coconut and pecans. Pour into 4 to 5-quart (4 L) slow cooker.

- Cover and cook on LOW for 3 to 4 hours or on HIGH 1 hour 30 minutes to 2 hours or until knife inserted into middle comes out clean.

TIP: Serve pudding warm with caramel ice cream topping, if desired.

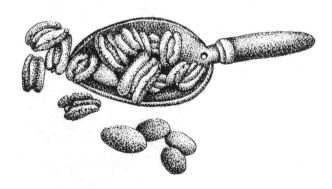

Butter-Baked Apples

6 large green baking apples	
¼ cup (½ stick) butter, melted	**60 ml**
2 tablespoons lemon juice	**30 ml**
1 cup packed brown sugar	**240 ml**
1 teaspoon cinnamon	**5 ml**
½ teaspoon nutmeg	**2 ml**

- Peel, core, cut apples in half and place in slow cooker.

- Drizzle with lemon juice and butter. Sprinkle with sugar and spices.

- Cover and cook on LOW for 2 hours 30 minutes to 3 hours 30 minutes or on HIGH for 1 hour 30 minutes to 2 hours.

Fresh Peach Cobbler

1 cup sugar	240 ml
¾ cup baking mix	180 ml
2 eggs	
2 teaspoons vanilla	10 ml
1 (5 ounce) can evaporated milk	143 g
2 tablespoons butter, melted	30 ml
3 large, ripe peaches, mashed	

- In large bowl, combine sugar and baking mix, stir in egg, vanilla, evaporated milk and butter and mix well.

- Fold in peaches, pour into sprayed slow cooker and stir well.

- Cover and cook on LOW for 6 to 8 hours or on HIGH for 3 to 4 hours. Serve warm with peach ice cream.

Peaches with Crunch

¾ cup old-fashioned oats	180 ml
⅓ cup packed brown sugar	160 ml
¾ cup granulated sugar	180 ml
½ cup baking mix	120 ml
½ teaspoon ground cinnamon	2 ml
2 (15 ounce) cans sliced peaches, well drained	2 (425 g)

- Lightly sprayed 3 or 4-quart (3 L) slow cooker. In bowl, combine oats, sugars, baking mix and cinnamon.

- Stir in drained peaches and spoon into slow cooker.

- Cover and cook on LOW for 4 to 5 hours. Serve in sherbet dishes.

Pineapple-Rice Pudding

1 cup cooked white rice	240 ml
¾ cup sugar	180 ml
1 (1 pint) carton half-and-half cream	.5 kg
1 tablespoon cornstarch	15 ml
3 eggs, beaten	
1 teaspoon vanilla	5 ml
1 (15 ounce) can crushed pineapple with juice	425 g

- In mixing bowl combine rice, sugar and half-and-half cream and mix well.

- Stir in cornstarch, eggs, vanilla and pineapple.

- Pour into sprayed 4 to 5-quart (4 L) slow cooker.

- Cover and cook on LOW for 2 to 3 hours.

- When ready to serve, top each serving with toasted, chopped pecans as a special touch.

Surprise Dessert

1 (18 ounce) box spice cake mix	510 g
1 cup butterscotch chips	240 ml
4 eggs, slightly beaten	
¾ cup oil	180 ml
1 (3.4 ounce) package butterscotch instant pudding mix	100 g
1 (8 ounce) carton sour cream	227 g
1 cup chopped pecans	240 ml

- Lightly sprayed 4 to 5-quart (4 to 5 L) slow cooker. In large bowl, combine all ingredients and ¾ cup (180 ml) water. Pour into cooker.

- Cover and cook on LOW for 6 to 7 hours or on HIGH for 3 hours to 3 hours 30 minutes. Serve hot or room temperature with butter-pecan ice cream.

Chocolate Delight

1 (18 ounce) box chocolate cake mix	510 g
1 (8 ounce) carton sour cream	227 g
4 eggs	
¾ cup oil	180 ml
1 (3.4 ounce) box instant chocolate pudding mix	100 g
¾ cup chopped pecans	180 ml

- Spray sides and bottom of slow cooker.

- In bowl mix cake mix, sour cream, eggs, oil, pudding mix, pecans and 1 cup (240 ml) water. Pour into slow cooker.

- Cover and cook on LOW for 6 to 8 hours.

- Serve hot or warm with vanilla ice cream.

Chocolate Fondue
Use the slow cooker as a fondue pot.

2 (7 ounce) chocolate bars, chopped	**2 (198 g)**
4 ounces white chocolate bar, chopped	**114 g**
1 (7 ounce) jar marshmallow creme	**(198 g**
¾ cup half-and-half cream	**180 ml**
½ cup slivered almonds, chopped, toasted	**120 ml**
¼ cup Amaretto®	**60 ml**
Pound cake	

- Combine broken chocolate bars, white chocolate bar, marshmallow creme, half-and-half cream and almonds in small, sprayed slow cooker.

- Cover and cook on LOW for about 2 hours or until chocolates melt. Stir to mix well and fold in Amaretto®.

TIP: Use slow cooker as fondue pot or transfer chocolate mixture to fondue pot. Cut pound cake into small squares and use to dip into fondue.

Cran-Apples for Pound Cake

1 (6 ounce) package dried apples	168 g
½ cup Craisins®	
3 cups cranberry juice cocktail	710 ml
¾ cup packed brown sugar	180 ml
2 cinnamon sticks, halved	

- Spray 3 to 4-quart (4 L) slow cooker and add apples, Craisins®, juice, brown sugar and cinnamon sticks.

- Cover and cook on LOW for 4 to 5 hours or until liquid absorbs and fruit is tender.

- Serve warm, at room temperature or chilled over slices of pound cake or vanilla ice cream.

Fruit Sauce

8 cups fresh fruit, thinly sliced	2 L
1 cup orange juice	240 ml
⅓ cup packed brown sugar	80 ml
⅓ cup sugar	80 ml
2 tablespoons quick-cooking tapioca	30 ml
1 teaspoon grated fresh ginger	5 ml
⅓ cup dried cranberries or cherries	160 ml

- In 4-quart (4 L) slow cooker combine fruit, juice, sugars, tapioca and ginger. Cover and cook on LOW for 4 hours. Add cranberries or cherries and mix well.

- Cover and let stand for 10 to 15 minutes. To serve, spoon over slices of pound cake or ice cream.

Magnificent Fudge

2 (16 ounce) jars slightly salted, dry-roasted peanuts	2 (.5 kg)
1 (12 ounce) package semi-sweet chocolate chips	340 g
1 (4 ounce) bar German chocolate, broken	114 g
2 (24 ounce) packages white chocolate bark or (3 pounds) almond bark, chopped	680 g/1.3 kg

- Place peanuts in sprayed 5-quart (5 L) slow cooker. In layers, add chocolate chips, German chocolate and white chocolate bark.

- Cover and cook on LOW for 3 hours without removing lid. When candy cooks 3 hours, remove lid, stir and cool in covered slow cooker. Stir again and drop by teaspoon onto wax paper.

TIP: For darker fudge, use 1 white bark and 1 dark bark. DO NOT STIR.

INDEX

INDEX

INDEX

Cookbooks Published by Cookbook Resources, LLC
Bringing Family and Friends to the Table

**cookbook
resources** LLC
Your Ultimate Source for Easy Cookbooks

www.cookbookresources.com

Easy

SLOW COOKER

COOKBOOK

Simple Ingredients and Easy Preparation
for Hassle-Free
Cooking

Barbara C. Jones

www.cookbookresources.com

cookbook resources LLC